Gone Wild

David Karlins

with Bruce K. Hopkins

WILEY

Wiley Publishing, Inc.

Adobe® Illustrator® CS2

Adobe® Illustrator® CS2 Gone Wild

Published by
Wiley Publishing, Inc.
111 River Street
Hoboken, N.J. 07030
www.wiley.com

Copyright © 2005 by Wiley Publishing, Inc., Indianapolis, Indiana

Published simultaneously in Canada

ISBN: 0-7645-9859-7

Manufactured in the United States of America

10 9 8 7 6 5 4 3 2 1

1K/QT/RQ/QV/IN

For general information on our other products and services or to obtain technical support, please contact our Customer Care Department within the U.S. at (800) 762-2974, outside the U.S. at (317) 572-3993 or fax (317) 572-4002.

Wiley also publishes its books in a variety of electronic formats. Some content that appears in print may not be available in electronic books.

Library of Congress Control Number: 2005926043

About the Authors

David Karlins is a graphic and interactive design consulting, teacher, and author. His books include *Digital Sports Photography: Take Winning Shots Every Time* by Serge Timacheff, *Total Digital Photography: The Shoot to Print Workflow Handbook*, and *PC Magazine Printing Great Digital Photos*.

David teaches Illustrator, web design, and digital video at San Francisco State University Multimedia Studies Center. Visit him at www.davidkarlins.com, as well as this book's web site, www.illustratorgonewild.com.

Lead illustrator **Bruce Hopkins** has been working as a freelance illustrator since 1989. His illustration work has worked has morphed over time from textile design to digital illustration for technical manuals. Bruce has pioneered the use of Illustrator in fine artwork, ranging from "Space" series (done with Adobe Illustrator) to landscapes (both real and imaginary), and traditional figure studies. Check out his site, www.bkhopkins.com.

Credits

Acquisitions Editor
Michael Roney

Project Editor
Timothy J. Borek

Technical Editor
Bruce Hopkins

Copy Editor
Nancy Rapoport

Editorial Manager
Robyn Siesky

Vice President & Group Executive Publisher
Richard Swadley

Vice President & Publisher
Barry Pruett

Project Coordinator
Maridee Ennis

Book Designer
LeAndra Hosier

Graphics and Production Specialists
Joyce Haughey
Jennifer Heleine
Lynsey Osborn

Quality Control Technician
Brian H. Walls

Proofreading and Indexing
TECHBOOKS Production Services

Dedicated to the memory of my Aunt LuVay Karlins,
a free thinker, and a rebel in her own way

Preface

This is a different kind of book about Adobe Illustrator CS2. Everyone involved was on a mission to do something unique. The underlying theme was pushing Illustrator in new directions, and into new dimensions.

Why? Because the tasks, features, and tricks that you discover when you go down the dark alleys and through the "Road Closed" signs in Illustrator will help you with whatever level or type of project in which you are involved. Illustrator's tools for mapping artwork onto 3D effects, for example, are far from intuitive, but they open up a whole range of design options that can be used in everything from architectural renderings to newsletters. Illustrator's fill options are almost limitless, and in this book you learn how to use them to enhance illustrations ranging from space backgrounds and pattern designs to comic book fills.

I was not bound, in writing this book, to promote whatever features Adobe wants to market with this upgrade of Illustrator. Nevertheless, Illustrator CS2's new Live Paint and Live Trace features are genuinely radical enhancements to the program, and readers who want to see how to use those features will find a variety of experiments and examples that explore the limits of both those features. At the same time, I drew on many years of teaching and the experiences of veteran illustrators to include projects in this book that rely on the most basic fundamentals of Illustrator to create eye-popping and interesting artwork.

In short, I think you'll find this book an odd synthesis of weird and functional, offbeat and practical, advanced and accessible.

This book does not pretend to provide a complete reference guide to Illustrator. Still, I strongly suspect that many designers will find this book a more fun and interesting way to learn Illustrator than memorizing facts in a reference guide. As a way of supplementing the materials in this book, I've provided substantial Illustrator reference material at the book's web site, www.illustratorgonewild.com. In addition to links and reference material, illustratorgonewild.com has scalable, vector versions of almost all the projects in this book. The book's web site, illustratorgonewild.com, is a work in progress, and I will add insights, rants, and observations while you read the book.

Finally, a word on how to navigate your way through the tasks (projects) in this book. There is certain logic to the order of the chapters, but feel free to skip around and do them in any order you wish. Many chapters involve projects that build on a previous project, so you'll find it a little easier if you work through the projects within a chapter in order.

Nearly all of the Tasks in this book are highly flexible. When I say apply one color, you can apply another. If I say scale it to one size, you can make it bigger or smaller. Where I suggest some text message, you can change that. In general, the more comfortable you are with Illustrator, the more you can freelance with the details in each project. Or, if you're teaching yourself Illustrator from scratch and using this book to do so, you'll want to stick to the script more carefully — at least at first. Another unique thing about this Illustrator book is that you are supposed to have fun working your way through it!

Acknowledgments

Thanks to the team who put this book together: Timothy J. Borek, project editor at Wiley, acquisitions editor Mike Roney, my courageous agent Margot Maley Hutchison at Waterside Productions, technical editor Bruce K. Hopkins, and the rest of the editorial and production crews at Wiley.

In addition to the artwork provided by lead illustrator Bruce K. Hopkins, car and motorcycle illustration guru Chris Nielsen was cool enough to let me use his motorcycle and portrait work in Tasks in this book.

Most especially, I need to acknowledge all the students I've had in my Illustrator classes over the years. Their questions, insights, complaints, and discoveries fuel my zeal for understanding, exploring, and stretching the limits of Illustrator.

Contents

THE RULES CHANGED !!

four bipolar photo effects **88**

five fresh outta the blender **108**

Contents

eleven wild web and animation

Contents

all wound up: 3d rotation and extrusion

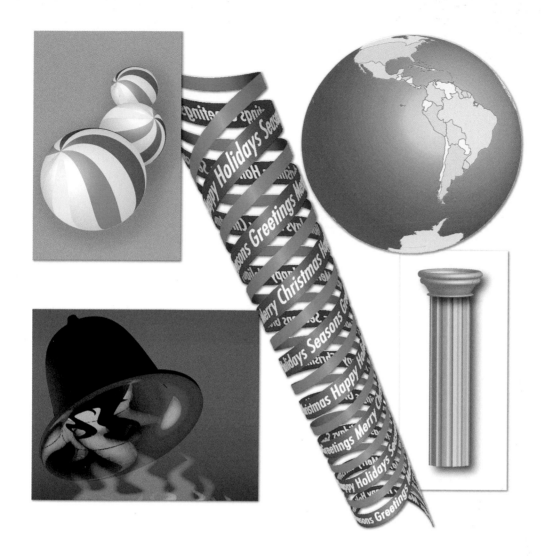

Illustrator *type* cannot be mapped, but in this chapter I show you how to get around that roadblock. I also confront the problem of sizing type to wrap correctly – without having letters cut off when the text wraps around the spiral. I show you a secret for doing that, and in the process raise your appreciation level for the importance of the value of pi!

If you find these projects tempting, but the tasks a bit beyond the pale, you might want to check out some of the basic Illustrator resources at www.illustratorgonewild.com, and then come back and hit them again. Also, before takeoff, check your RAM. 3D effects are as taxing on processor resources as almost anything else in Illustrator CS2. Anything less than 1 gigabyte (GB) of RAM on your machine, and the effects involved in this project take maddeningly long. Higher processor speed will also improve performance when you work with 3D effects, and in general, PCs require faster processing and more RAM than Macs for working with graphics. In any event, anything less than 1GB of RAM, your computer will be gasping for air.

You've been warned. So, if you're ready to live on the wild side of Illustrator, strap on your helmet and let's go.

Mapping Type on a Spiral

Here's a fun, challenging project that goes deep into little-explored realms of Illustrator's 3D mapping features. This "Happy Holidays" illustration takes advantage of Illustrator CS2's ability to map objects on a revolved or extruded shape.

Often 3D-generated effects use one of the available generated surfaces (like plastic shading) for the final object. I break convention here by using the wireframe surface, generating 3D effects with a strippable "skin" so to speak. The 3D mapping provides the grid for the spiraling type and stripes.

(1) Start by drawing a 2-inch circle with no stroke. The circle will be extruded later, and — like many of the objects you generate in this project — will be stripped off like scaffolding to reveal the final project.

CAUTION

It's important that the circle have no stroke applied. Otherwise, it will create a pipe-like tube with more (inside) surface, which you don't want for this project.

(2) Draw a rectangular stripe with a length the circumference of the circle and thickness to taste. We're creating a stripe that wraps, candy cane–like, around a cylinder we generate using 3D effects.

(3) Add another, contrasting color stripe, and duplicate the two stripes to create a repeating stripe pattern. The length of the repeating pattern isn't critical to the project: A height of 7 inches will work fine.

TIP

The circumference of the circle? You calculate the circumference of (distance around) a circle by multiplying the diameter (width across the middle) by a value referred to as π (or "pi"). Mathematicians are still straining to calculate the exact value of pi, but for our purposes, rounding off to 3.14 will do fine. In this case, our rectangle should be about 6.28" long. For an existential perspective of the psychological, corporate, repressive, and mystical aspects of the search for the final value of pi (and, correspondingly, additional insights into this project), rent the DVD *Pi* (1988, starring Sean Gullette). Just don't let "them" know you're renting it!

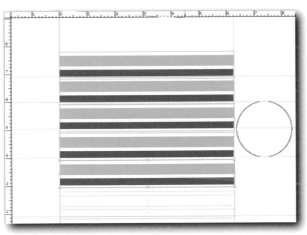

TIP

One trick for quickly and evenly duplicating the two bars is to place them in a rectangle with no fill or stroke. Arrange the two horizontal bars (the green and red bars) on top of the invisible rectangle, and vertically center them. Then just use Command/Ctrl-click and drag to duplicate rectangles below the original.

Don't worry, at this point, about exactly what colors to assign to the rectangles or the type. Unfortunately, the colors are lost during the process of generating a 3D effect, and you restore them in the final stages of this project. The point of assigning colors now is to help you envision how the project will look at the end.

NOTE

Outline type is, of course, not editable, and were this a basic reference book on Illustrator, I'd insert an appropriate lecture on the pros (flexibility, transferability) and cons (non–editability) of converting type to outlines. Given that we're halfway down the advanced slope, no need for warnings like that right now, but *do* do a bit of research before you start making a principle of converting non–backed up type to outlines!

4 Create text, and use the Character palette to define font and type size to fit type to the horizontal bars. To duplicate the text content in this project, use the text content shown here. Or . . . not. You can experiment with your own message!

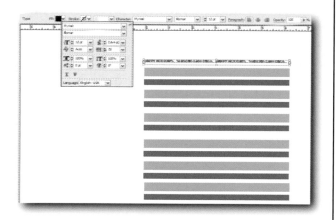

5 Center the text. To quickly and easily select all type, choose Select ➪ Objects ➪ Text Objects. Then, you *can* use the Align Center tool in the Paragraph panel to center the type. But you might get better results just eye-balling (using the right/left arrow keys to adjust horizontal type positioning) because type boxes don't always reflect the actual margins of the type.

6 With the text still selected, convert the type to outlines by choosing Type ➪ Create Outlines. Apply a white fill using the Fill icon in the Tools box.

SHORTCUT

Using vertical guides (dragged from the vertical ruler onto the artboard), and turning on Snap to Point (from the View menu) make it easy to maintain the width of the skewed rectangles and text. Another approach is to use horizontal guides, so you can place one on the bottom, and one on the top of a corresponding stripe and then skew. If you do that, remember to place the skew center point on the bottom-left corner of the stripes.

7 Select the whole project — the horizontal rectangles and text that has been converted to outlines — and group everything (Command/Ctrl+G). Use the Sheer tool to skew the repeating stripes. Drag on the lower-left anchor of the grouped objects to maintain the calculated width of the pattern. This makes a repeating strip that fits on the extrude circle.

8 Rather than worry about whether the type and stripe objects are long enough to map on the cylinder we'll soon generate, duplicate the skewed object so that the it is 24 inches long or so.

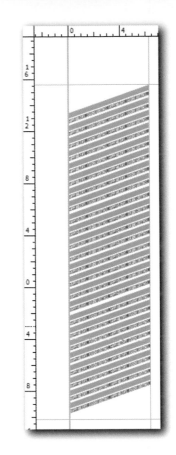

9 In order to map an object onto a generated 3D effect, the object first has to be converted into a symbol. Select everything, and turn the object into a symbol by dragging it into the Symbol palette. You might want to double-click on the new symbol and give it a better name: Stripes. Feel free to come up with another name, but make a note of it because you'll need it when you map the artwork on to the cylinder.

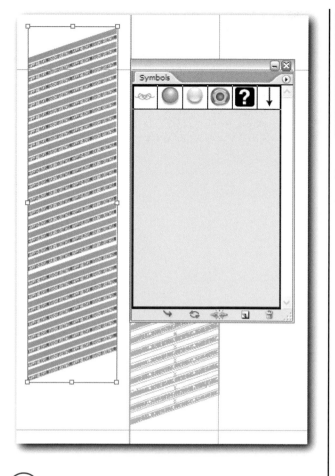

TIP

If your computer is becoming too sluggish while defining extrude and bevel options, clear the Preview checkbox. You won't be able to interactively see the effect applied to the cylinder. You can periodically check (and then uncheck) the Preview checkbox to look at the effect in the artboard.

11 Apply the following settings in the 3D Extrude & Bevel Options dialog box to generate the cylinder that will provide a structure for the helix:

* **Extrude depth:** 1000 pts

* **Position:** Off axis left to define the direction of the extrusion

* **Perspective:** 160 degrees for a tightly defined extrusion

* Select Wireframe from the Surface popup to create a bare stroked outline instead of a textured surface

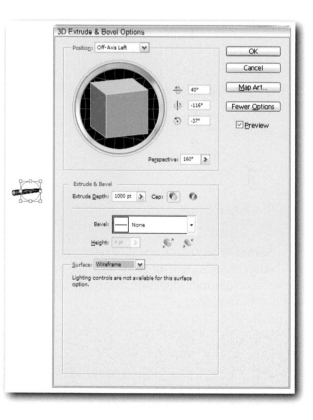

10 The pieces are in place. You've created the artwork to be mapped. Now it's show time! Select the 2-inch circle you drew (in Step 1), and launch the 3D Extrude & Bevel Options dialog box by selecting Effect ⮕ 3D ⮕ Extrude & Bevel. Click the More Options button if necessary to display the entire dialog box. Turn on Preview by clicking the checkbox, and position the 3D Extrude & Bevel Options dialog box so you can see your 2-inch circle on the artboard as you apply effects.

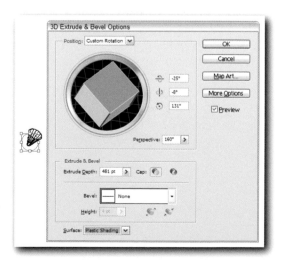

12 To map the symbol, click the Map Art button. The Map Art dialog box opens (and the 3D Extrude & Bevel Options dialog box stays open). There are three surfaces for this cylinder: the top two surfaces are the ends, and the third is the side (length) of the cylinder. Use the direction arrows in the Surface area of the dialog box to navigate to Surface 3 of 3.

The Symbol drop-down list displays all symbols saved with this Illustrator CS2 file. Choose the Stripes symbol you created in Step 9. The Map Art dialog box has its own Preview checkbox you can select or clear to display the mapping interactively in the artboard (or not).

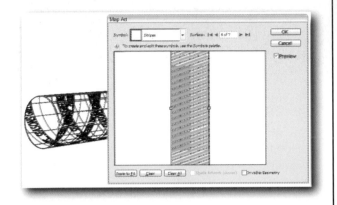

13 Click OK to add the mapped art to the effect, and to close the Map Art dialog box. Click OK to close the 3D Extrude & Bevel Options dialog box and apply the 3D effect to what was once a humble 2-inch circle.

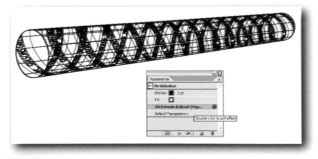

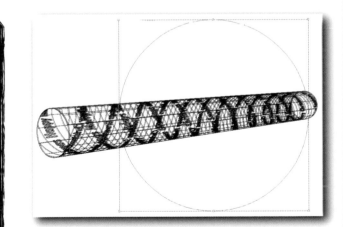

The original circle, from which you generated the cylindrical tube, is no longer visible as the 3D effect process stripped the original shape of its fill and stroke. The circle is visible only because it is selected, and I am displaying the bounding box (use Shift+Command/Ctrl+B to toggle display of the bounding box on or off). You could also see the original circle in Outline view (toggle back and forth between Preview and Outline view with Command/Ctrl+Y). Interestingly, the tube, with mapped artwork, does *not* appear in Outline view. That's because it doesn't "really" exist! The entire project is a generated effect.

As long as the artwork is an effect, you can easily adjust the effect settings by opening the effect dialog box by double-clicking the effect in the Appearances palette. The Appearances palette associates with a selected object (in this case the original, no-longer-visible circle).

In the next step of this project, you abandon the option of tweaking 3D effects. It is necessary to change the effect into an object for final cleanup and editing. Consider, then, the option of saving your file now as a backup so you can return to the effect at will. Or, duplicate the object, and proceed with just one file. Either way provides you with a backup.

14 Expand the appearance of the effect by selecting the circle and choosing Object ➪ Expand Appearance. Now you can edit the object like any other set of vectors.

15 It's cleanup time. You need to remove unwanted shapes left over from the wireframe imposed by the effect process. You also need to perform several levels of ungrouping (Shift+Command/Ctrl+G) on the object until you can easily select the wireframe and delete it.

SHORTCUT

You can reduce the sweat you pour into the final touchup by honing your selection skills. Part of the trick is to ungroup the expanded object *just enough* to allow you to select the objects you need to delete or edit, without ungrouping so much that you can edit only by selecting every letter or stripe individually.

Another helpful selection technique is to use the Select ⇨ Same option from the dialog box to select objects of similar stroke width. Regardless of your selection skills, the final colorizing is one of those things that makes digital illustration the crazy, time-consuming process that it is. You'll need to resort to the Direct Selection tool for elements of the illustration.

16 Before you hit the showers, do final touchup on the project. Select the type and add colors. Do the same with the stripes. Rotate, resize, and crop the spiral.

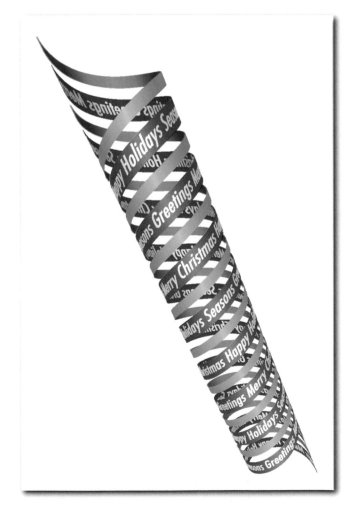

Einstein in 3D

Among his insights into Einstein's contributions, Brian Green has said that "Einstein taught us that geometry and physics are very tightly woven together." Follow this thread at the web site for the Nova series *The Elegant Universe* (www.pbs.org/wgbh/nova/elegant/).

In tribute to that contribution, let's apply Illustrator's 3D mapping features to *sphericize* Einstein's portrait by mapping his face onto a revolved object. The before and after images are shown here.

Before plunging into this . . . *sphere* . . . of Illustrator, a few additional notes on using 3D Effects. *Ancianos* (wise elders) will recall elements of these 3D Effects from another life when they existed in the form of Adobe Dimensions. Some, but not all, of the features of Dimensions evolved into 3D Effects, while others . . . unfortunately Illustrator has yet to incorporate the full 3D generation functionality of Dimensions.

Because Illustrator CS2's 3D generation operates as *effects,* you don't actually generate objects. If you tried Task 1, you noted that when viewed in Outline view, the 3D cylinder didn't even really exist (another tribute to Einstein?). The *appearance* of the 3D effect had to be transformed and it was necessary to *expand* the effect to transform it into editable curves for final touches. We'll recycle the trick of generating 3D effects and then expanding them in this, and other, 3D projects.

In this task, you use Illustrator CS2's new interactive trace features to convert a JPEG of Einstein into a vector image. Feel free, of course, to trace your own raster artwork for mapping, or just start with vector art. In any case, you convert that vector art into a symbol to allow it to be mapped, and apply it to a revolved hemisphere. You'll see . . .

NOTE

Other evolutionary branches of the accessible 3D software tree are products from Curious Labs One inexpensive 3D generation option is MagicalSketch 2 (www.curiouslabs.com), which is marketed as a kid's illustration program, but works for basic 3D shape generation. Shade 7 designer LE is a more full-featured 3D generation package, also available from Curious Labs. Seven-day demo versions can be downloaded for free.

Well-organized graphic artists (is that an oxymoron?) assign a coherent name to the symbol by double clicking on the symbol in the Symbols palette. Others don't.

(1) Start by finding a JPEG of Einstein, or your own portrait photo. Open a new file in Illustrator, and Choose File ⇨ Place (and navigate to and select your photo). With the photo on the artboard and selected, Illustrator CS2 automatically displays the Live Trace Control palette to trace the objects and convert it to vectors.

(2) After you clean up the expanded, traced image, group the vectors that were generated by the trace.

(3) Turn the grouped, vectorized artwork into a symbol by dragging it (all) into the Symbols palette.

(4) With the symbol safely stashed in the Symbols palette (and, thus, available for mapping when you generate a sphere), draw a semicircle. Unlike the mapping experience you might have enjoyed in Task 1, size doesn't matter here in creating a mapped object. That's because instead of precisely wrapping type around a cylinder, you'll be slapping a face on a sphere, and sizing it to fit during the 3D mapping process.

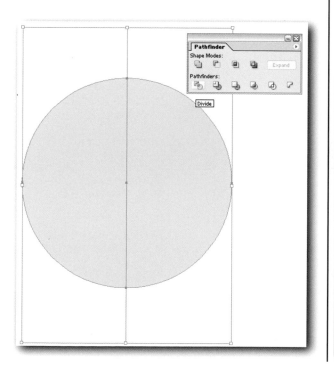

(5) With the semicircle selected, open the 3D Revolve Options dialog box by choosing Effect ⇨ 3D ⇨ Revolve. Apply settings as shown here

* Set rotation to 360° for a complete rotation.
* Set Position to Front.
* Set Offset to 0 pts and Left Edge.
* From the Surface drop-down menu, choose No Shading.
* Set Perspective to 100°.
* Don't click OK yet! You still have to map the portrait.

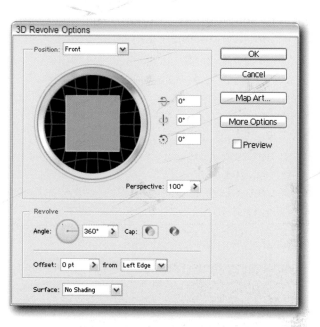

Mental Health Tips

There is only one surface here (no top, bottom, and so on), so don't spend a long time agonizing over which surface to choose from the Surface drop-down list.

Also, if the placement of the head on the grid in the Map Art dialog box doesn't seem to match the location of the artwork on the previewed effect, it's not a perception issue on your part. Illustrator CS2 seems to have inherited at least some of the bugginess of Illustrator CS in that mapped objects always appear substantially higher on the mapping grid in the dialog box than they actually appear when the effect is generated. You'll want to move Einstein's (or whoever's) head so high on the mapping grid that it looks like his head is over the top of the sphere.

You can also rotate the sphere by dragging the cube in the 3D dialog box or entering numbers to the right of the cube rather than worrying about placement in the mapping dialog box.

Enhancing the Background

To provide a left brain/right brain effect, create a separate background semicircle. Apply a psychedelic gradient to the semicircle, and move it behind the outline. You can further tune the image by applying fill colors and transparency to the figure itself. Try playing with stroke attributes for the portrait—heavier stroke weights can have a dramatic impact on the illustration.

TIP

Locate the symbol so the entire image appears in the visible section of the mapping surface. Both Windows and OS X (shown below) display mapped objects higher in the Map Art dialog box grid than the artwork actually will appear in the generated effect.

6 To map the Einstein symbol to the surface of the sphere, click the Map Art button. The Map Art dialog box opens. Choose the symbol you created (but may well not have bothered to name) in Step 3 from the Symbol drop-down menu. Size your symbol (by clicking and dragging on the sizing handles) and locate it as shown here.

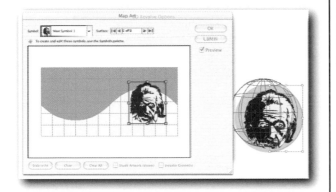

7 Generate the sphere with the mapped artwork by clicking OK twice to close the Map Art and 3D Revolve Options dialog boxes.

8 As foreshadowed in the intro to this project, you'll usually want to have more fun with mapped symbols than is allowed with the artwork constrained in a 3D effect. It's necessary, now, to break the illustration out of the 3D mold so we can fine-tune fills and strokes. Do that by selecting the generated 3D effect and choosing Object ➪ Expand Appearance. The result is a highly grouped bunch of vectors.

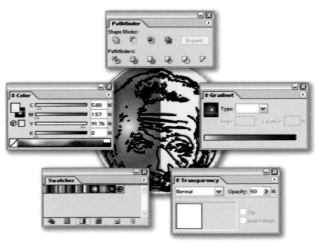

(**9**) Apply a suitably trippy gradient fill (you can find pre-fab ones in the Swatches panel), and an appropriately contrasting stroke color to the expanded vector object.

Making Marbles

As with most of our 3D mapping excursions, this task has two basic phases: First, you create mappable artwork and turn it into a symbol. In this case, the mapped symbol becomes the stripes on a marble.

Second, you revolve an object into a 3D effect — in this case a spherical marble. And you map the artwork on the revolved 3D effect. Was that three phases? Or two phases and a sub-phase? You be the judge.

At any rate, with some imagination, you come away from this project with techniques you can use for beach balls, barber poles, pinwheels, and a whole myriad of spirally thingies.

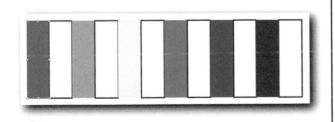

1 Create a rectangle. Dimensions aren't particularly important, but to follow the model here, make the rectangle 0.25 inches wide, and 0.75 inches high. Or so. Apply a bright color fill.

2 Duplicate on the right side to make 12 sections. Assign fun colors to the odd-numbered rectangles (first, third . . .).

Here's an alternative way to duplicate the rectangle: Hold down Option/Alt key while using the Group Selection tool to click and drag one corner point of the rectangle until it touches another point of the rectangle. Duplicated! Then press Command/Ctrl+D to repeat the process as many times as necessary.

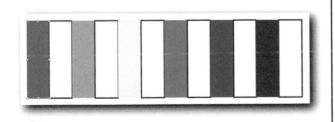

3 Draw a rectangle with no stroke or fill around all 12 rectangles.

4 Delete the even numbered rectangles (the second, fourth, sixth, and eighth). Assign temporary colors to the other rectangles.

> ## TIP
>
> A technique to make it easier to duplicate, space, and align the rectangles: Turn on Snap to Point (Option/Alt+ Command/Ctrl+") to facilitate placing rectangles next to each other, and turn on Smart Guides (Command/Ctrl+U); then use Option/Alt+ click and drag to generate new rectangles in place. Or, you might find vertical alignment easier with a Horizontal Guide displayed (drag down a ruler).
>
> To steroidize the impact of Snap to Point in forcing your rectangles to align and be contiguous (touching), crank up the Snapping tolerance. Do that by choosing Illustrator/ Edit ⇨ Preferences ⇨ Smart Guides & Slides. Entering the max value (10 pts) generates intense onscreen magnetism making it simple to align objects to a gridline or snap them next to each other. Maxing out the snap tolerance is helpful when you want to easily snap objects together, and you're not planning to work with a bunch of objects that *almost* touch but don't.

5 Direct select all top points of the remaining rectangles. Don't select the enclosing rectangles. Using the bounding rectangle as a guide, drag the selected points to the right to skew the rectangles.

6 Duplicate and reposition the parallelograms you created from skewed rectangles so that you double the length of the set of bars. Reposition the invisible rectangle so it can be used to crop the stripes. Cut out a rectangle from the stripes by selecting everything and pressing Option/Alt and clicking the Subtract from Shape Area in the Pathfinder palette.

TIP

As is the case with wavelength subatomic particles, or objects only visible with the assistance of hallucinogens, this rectangle with no stroke or fill is invisible (when not selected), at least in Preview view. Toggle over to Outline view (Command/Ctrl+Y) to select and manipulate the outer rectangle.

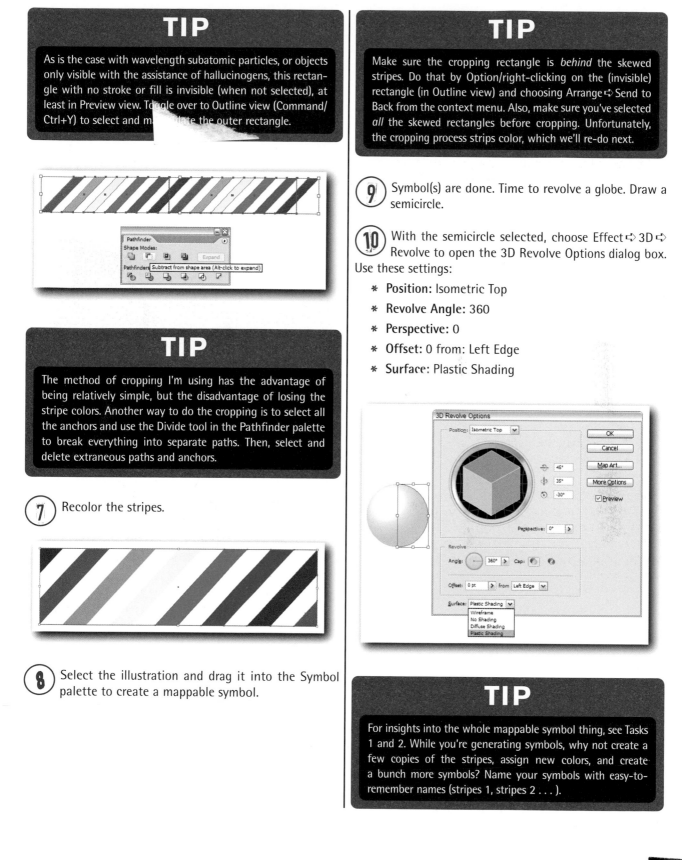

TIP

The method of cropping I'm using has the advantage of being relatively simple, but the disadvantage of losing the stripe colors. Another way to do the cropping is to select all the anchors and use the Divide tool in the Pathfinder palette to break everything into separate paths. Then, select and delete extraneous paths and anchors.

(7) Recolor the stripes.

(8) Select the illustration and drag it into the Symbol palette to create a mappable symbol.

TIP

Make sure the cropping rectangle is *behind* the skewed stripes. Do that by Option/right-clicking on the (invisible) rectangle (in Outline view) and choosing Arrange ⇨ Send to Back from the context menu. Also, make sure you've selected *all* the skewed rectangles before cropping. Unfortunately, the cropping process strips color, which we'll re-do next.

(9) Symbol(s) are done. Time to revolve a globe. Draw a semicircle.

(10) With the semicircle selected, choose Effect ⇨ 3D ⇨ Revolve to open the 3D Revolve Options dialog box. Use these settings:

- ✳ **Position:** Isometric Top
- ✳ **Revolve Angle:** 360
- ✳ **Perspective:** 0
- ✳ **Offset:** 0 from: Left Edge
- ✳ **Surface:** Plastic Shading

TIP

For insights into the whole mappable symbol thing, see Tasks 1 and 2. While you're generating symbols, why not create a few copies of the stripes, assign new colors, and create a bunch more symbols? Name your symbols with easy-to-remember names (stripes 1, stripes 2 . . .).

11 Click the Map Art button to open the Map Art dialog box. Don't worry about placing the mapped art using the grid in the Map Art dialog box. That doesn't really work that well anyway (see Task 5). Instead, simply click the Scale to Fit button to rescale the mapped art to fit the entire surface.

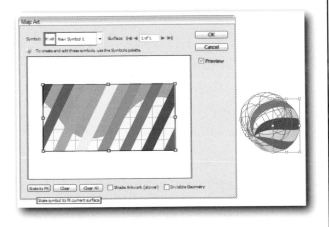

12 Click OK a couple times to generate the 3D effect. The mapped artwork now exists only as an effect that can't be edited. Expand appearance by selecting the entire generated marble and choosing Object ➪ Expand Appearance (you might want to create a backup copy first

so you can play with the rotation and mapping later). To clean up the expanded object for easier editing, ungroup it about a billion times (or so), and then view it in Outline view. Clean up all the unnecessary wireframe remaining from the 3D effect for easier editing.

13 Select the (now selectable) stripes with the Direct Selection tool, and fill most or all of them with radial gradients.

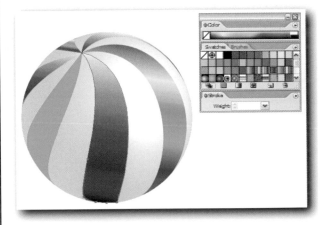

Doric Entablature

In this task, you construct a simplified Doric column by rotating two curves to create the column and top, or *entablature* of the column. Of the three main forms of Greek columns—Doric, Ionic, and Corinthian—the most basic was Doric. The famous Parthenon is probably the best-known example. Serge Timacheff, my co-author for Wiley's *Total Digital Photography . . .* series, captured the columns of the Parthenon while shooting the Olympic games in Greece. His photos will be of great assistance in generating a vectorized Greek column. The first phase of this project involves drawing a gear-like closed path, and then extruding that "slice" of the column to generate the column.

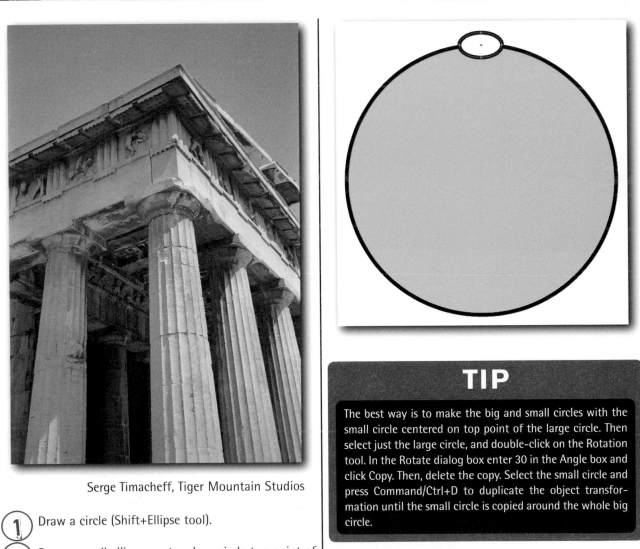

Serge Timacheff, Tiger Mountain Studios

① Draw a circle (Shift+Ellipse tool).

② Draw a small ellipse, centered on circle top point of the circle.

TIP

The best way is to make the big and small circles with the small circle centered on top point of the large circle. Then select just the large circle, and double-click on the Rotation tool. In the Rotate dialog box enter 30 in the Angle box and click Copy. Then, delete the copy. Select the small circle and press Command/Ctrl+D to duplicate the object transformation until the small circle is copied around the whole big circle.

③ Create duplicates of the small ellipse, placed along the circumference of the circle, spaced 30° apart.

(4) Select the entire project (so far) and click with the Live Paint tool to create a Live Paint group in the middle of the drawing.

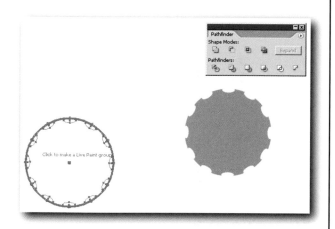

(5) Choose Object ➪ Expand to convert the Live Paint area into a path that can be extruded. If you used the Divide Pathfinder tool, deselect the center object and press delete to clean up the ellipses.

(6) Fill with a gray gradient fill.

(7) To extrude the selected path into a column, choose Effect ➪ 3D ➪ Extrude & Bevel. Apply the following settings in the Extrude & Bevel Options dialog box:

* **X Axis rotation:** –95°
* **Y Axis rotation:** 0°
* **Z Axis rotation:** 0°
* **Perspective:** 0°
* **Extrude Depth:** 225 pt
* **Cap:** On
* **Bevel:** No
* **Shading:** Plastic Surface

* **Shading Color:** Black
* **Light Intensity:** 100%
* **Ambient Light:** 50%
* **Highlight Intensity:** 60%
* **Highlight Size:** 90%
* **Blend Steps:** 25

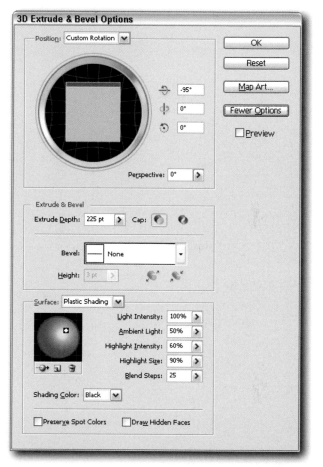

8 Click OK to apply the extrusion and generate the column.

To maintain some authenticity, you can find a photo or sketch of a Doric column on the web. Or . . . scan the one at the beginning of this chapter. Or . . . it will work fine to just fake it and draw a curve that roughly approximates Doric entablature. You will trace that section of the column to create a curve that will be revolved to generate a vectorized 3D column.

9 Use File ➪ Place to place a bitmap image of a Doric entablature on the artboard. Place the photo as a template layer for easier editing by checking the Template checkbox in the Place dialog box as you select the photo.

TIP

The outlined stroke with a fill provides more flexibility when applying surface lighting options in the 3D Revolve Options dialog box.

10 With the placed Doric entablature photo selected, use the Pen tool to create a smooth curve that *roughly* corresponds to the edge of the entablature. Draw the bottom of the curve as shown to facilitate a nice revolved effect. Or, fake it by not tracing anything, and drawing a curve similar to this one. Keep the anchor points smooth to generate a smoother 3D effect. Make the bottom segment of the curve *about* half the diameter of the generated column. You can adjust the width of the entablature to match the column after you generate the 3D revolved effect.

TIP

I manipulated a section of one of Serge's Parthenon photos to create an easy-to-trace entablature section of a column. That was a bit too much hassle. You'll find dozens of traceable images if you use the Images option in your favorite search engine, and look for "Doric Entablature."

11 Convert the curve you drew of a profile of the entablature to path by choosing Object ➪ Path ➪ Outline stroke. Apply a gray fill.

Why *Not* Trace?

I *so* wanted to use this as an opportunity to play with the new Live Trace button in the Object bar that you get when you select a bitmap in Illustrator CS2. I had a whole plan to tweak the Threshold slider until the interactive trace created a solid silhouette. That all worked, and was almost too easy. The only problem was it turned out to be much easier to trace the bitmap with the Pen tool than to edit the generated path. That's okay . . . we'll find more chances to play with tracing.

The other factor in choosing the Pen tool is that the curve needs to be as *simple* as possible. The more you experiment with revolved curves, the more you'll appreciate the usefulness of keeping those curves both *simple* and *smooth*. Reducing the number of anchors, and keeping curves smooth generates smoother, cleaner 3D revolved effects.

(12) With the shape you created by tracing the side (and half the bottom) of the entablature selected, choose Effect + 3D ➪ Revolve, and apply a setting of –5° X axis. The other 3D Revolve Options dialog box settings should be

* **Y Axis rotation:** 0°
* **Z Axis rotation:** 0°
* **Perspective:** 0°
* **Extrude Depth:** 225 point
* **Cap:** On
* **Bevel:** None
* **Shading:** Plastic Surface
* **Shading Color:** None

NOTE

The -5° X axis tilt here equals . . . the Leaning Tower of Pisa? Coincidentally, yes. But the point here is that the 5° tilt forward nicely simulates looking up at the entablature. And it coordinates with the angle we assigned to the column itself, so they should fit together okay. You can tweak the X axis tilt interactively in the 3D Revolve Options dialog box.

* **Light Intensity:** 100%
* **Ambient Light:** 30%
* **Highlight Intensity:** 30%
* **Highlight Size:** 90%
* **Blend Steps:** 25

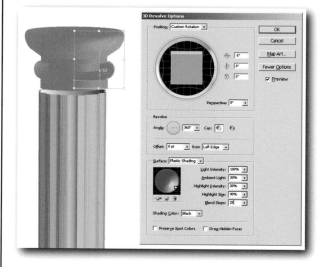

(13) After you create the column and the entablature, create a copy (so you can return to and edit the 3D effects). Tweak the size and placement of the entablature to match the column.

(14) For final touch-up, group both pieces of the project, and expand the appearance of the grouped objects.

The expanded project can be touched up — the fill colors can be fine-tuned, gradients applied if necessary. Or, just drop a little drop shadow on the project to finalize it.

TIP

By keeping an unexpanded copy of the project, you reserve the ability to edit the 3D effects using the Appearance palette.

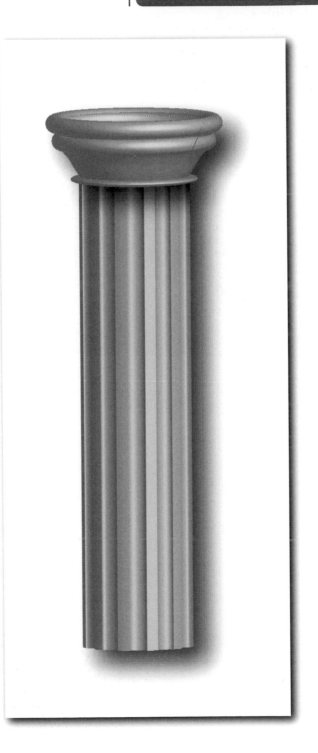

Hell's Bell Curve

A decade ago or so, some idiot wrote a book called *The Bell Curve* that supposedly produced "scientific" evidence that folks who have been institutionalized into the underclass were there because of their genes. In this Illustrator design project, however, you will create a *bell from a curve*. That's different, don't worry!

This 3D revolve project introduces a . . . *spin* on the technique of revolving a curve. The new trick here is that you map artwork *inside* as well as outside of a revolved shape. Specifically, you map flames onto the inside of a bell to simulate reflected fire inside the bell. The first step is to draw the curve that will be revolved to generate the bell. As with other rotated curve projects in this chapter, you outline the curve, transforming it first into a shape for better control over the revolve and mapping process.

1 Draw a curve that corresponds to the left edge of a silhouette of a bell.

TIP

The Butt cap option should be selected in the Stroke dialog box so that the curve has flat ends that don't extend and distort the curve.

2 Use the Stroke palette to assign a width of 10 pixels to the curve.

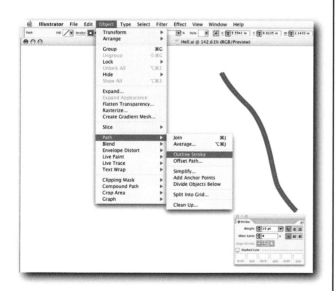

3 Convert the curve to a filled path.

TIP

To convert any stroke into a closed path (shape), choose Object ➪ Path ➪ Outline Stroke.

4 Assign a red fill, and no stroke color to the path.

You map the Fire symbol that comes with Illustrator CS2 onto both the outside and inside of the bell. You also use the symbol as part of the final illustration.

5 Choose Window ➪ Symbol Library ➪ Nature to open the Symbols library with fire, and drag the Fire symbol onto the artboard.

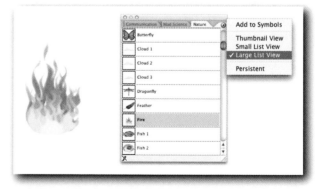

TIP

The shape is now ready to revolve into a bell. Keep it on the artboard; you'll return to it after you prepare mapping artwork.

6 Drag the Fire symbol into the regular Symbols palette so it is available to apply to the revolved bell. No need to rename the symbol — Fire is good.

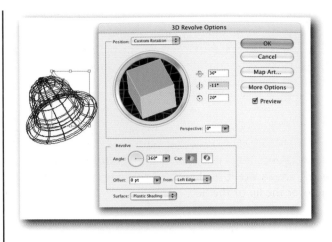

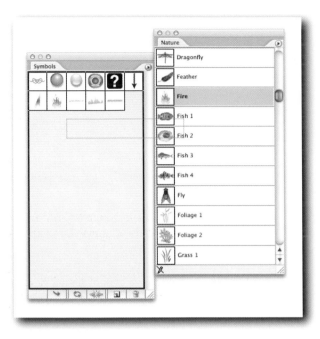

The next phase of the project is to generate the bell from the curve, and to map artwork to both the outside and inside of the bell.

7 With just your curve selected, choose Effects ⇨ 3D ⇨ Revolve to open the 3D Revolve Options dialog box.

8 Leave the angle set to the default value of 360 to generate a full (360 degree) rotated object. If your system resources support the Preview checkbox, play with X, Y, and Z rotation to generate a bell that tilts back, to the right, and up. If Preview is out of the question, or if you want some settings to start with, set X rotation to 36 degrees, Y rotation to –11 degrees, and Z rotation to 20 degrees.

9 The only other critical setting in the 3D Revolve Options dialog box at this point is to select the Plastic Shading surface. Darken the effect by reducing the Ambient Light setting to 0%.

10 Click the Map Art Symbol button in the 3D Revolve Options dialog box.

ALERT

Because of the semi-randomness of how mapping surfaces are generated, you need to rely on the Preview checkbox to determine which surfaces are mapping on the outside of the bell, and which surfaces are mapping on the inside.

11 The first mappable surface, surface 1, should be the inside of the bell. From the Symbol drop-down list, choose the Fire symbol. Click the Scale to Fit button in the Map Art dialog box, and then drag the symbol in the placement grid in the Map Art dialog box until the inside of the bell displays flickering flames.

12 Using the arrows next to the Surface list, navigate to the outside surface that maps onto the lip of the bell curve. Select the Fire symbol again as the mappable artwork, and locate it so that the flames appear to be licking up over the lip of the bell.

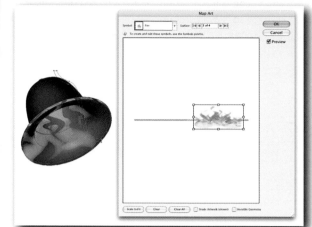

13 When the mapped artwork is visible on, and in the bell, click OK once to exit the Mapping Options dialog box.

14 Tweak lighting in the Surface area of the 3D Revolve Options dialog box to extenuate the lighting on the *inside* of the bell.

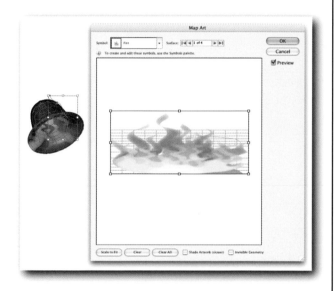

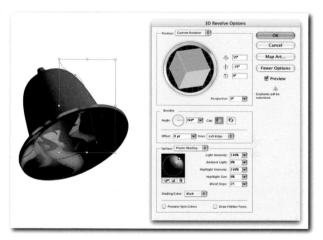

15 Click OK to close the 3D Revolve Options dialog box, and to generate the object.

You can emphasize the effect by using the Fire symbol below the bell, and adding a background behind the whole thing with a gradient. Other touchup tricks:

* Expand the appearance of the 3D effect and the symbol to touch up coloring.

* Apply some transparency to the flames from the Fire symbol.

* Use a rectangle to create a clipping mask to trim the final illustration.

Dripping Wax

Blends are integral to generating 3D effects. In this project, you use two different techniques to generate blends. You rotate half a candle to create a whole candle. Why is that a blend? Because the 3D revolve effect actually generates blends (and you can define how many steps in the blend in the 3D Revolve Options dialog box if you click the More Options button). You also use a couple smooth blends to generate three dimensionality, including blending two versions of the candle wick together to create a rich three-dimensional feel to the bent wick. Finally, you use a smooth blend to add a glow to the candle. When finished, you'll be ready to light up.

(1) Draw a rectangle about 0.6 inches wide, and about 6.25 inches high. This is the final width of the candle. In the next step, you slice it in half to prepare to revolve it, but here you're generating a rectangle that gives a sense of the final width.

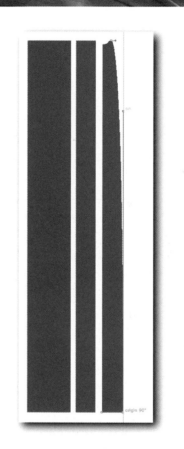

(2) Resize the rectangle to about half the original width (you can do this with the Selection tool). Use the Direct Selection tool to move anchors to change the rectangle into a trapezoid approximating the final half-candle shape.

ALTERNATIVE

First, draw a question mark–shaped open path (sure, you can use a real question mark type character and convert it to an outline). Apply the stroke width you want for the wick. Copy the path, and paste on top. Apply a thinner stroke to the copy. Select both stroked paths. Apply a smooth blend between them. There is no need to group the resulting blend; it's already grouped (blending does that). Copy the outside path, and paste it to the front. Fill the copy (in front) with a linear gradient. Finally, select the top linear gradient and in the Transparency palette select darken and give it a transparency of 65%.

(3) Use the Convert Anchor Point tool (Shift+C) to tweak the anchor handles at the top of the candle to generate half a concave curve that will be the top of the candle.

27

4 Use the Convert Anchor Point tool again on the anchor on the bottom-right corner of the candle to generate a smooth, rounded side for the candle.

5 Apply a simple 3D rotation effect to the selected half-candle. Choose Effect ⇨ 3D ⇨ Revolve. Apply –5 degrees X axis rotation.

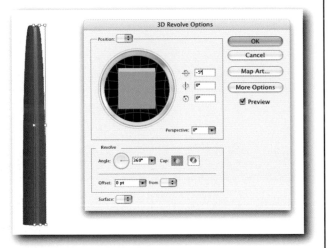

Since the beginning of this candle has a bit of a mystical 3D edge, why create a simple wick?

6 Start the wick by drawing a question mark–shaped closed path. Duplicate the shape. Make the second shape much thinner, but about the same height. Make the

TIP

Pay a bit of attention to the small "bulb" at the top of the drop. When the dripping wax is later applied to the candle, the bulb simulates the top of the candle overflowing down the side. Duplicate the drip, and resize the second drop to be almost the entire length, and about half the width of the original. Apply a dark brown fill to the larger drop, and a beige fill to the thinner fill.

thicker shape brown and the thinner shape white fill. Apply no stroke color to both shapes.

7 Place the thinner shape inside the thicker one. Group the two shapes.

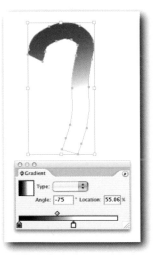

8 Create a copy of the larger wick shape, and fill it with a black-to-white gradient. Define the black to white gradient as a linear gradient with an angle of –75 degrees, and the white inkwell location at about 55%.

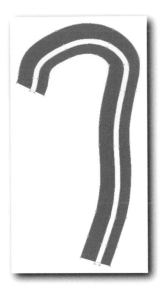

9 Move the grouped shape over the shape with the gradient fill. Select both shapes, and apply a smooth blend between them.

11 Simulating dripping wax adds a dimension of time to the illustration. The basic technique involves blending two drops. Use the Pen tool to draw a stream of dripped wax.

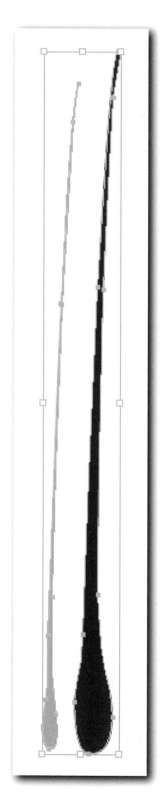

10 Draw a clipping mask around the wick to slice an irregular cut across the bottom. Select both the clipping mask and the wick, and select Object ⇨ Clipping Mask ⇨ Make.

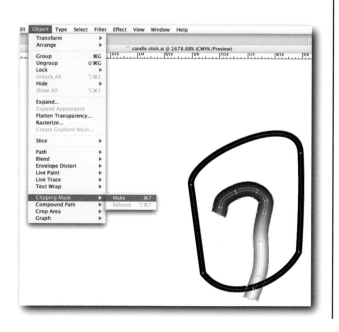

⑫ Move the thinner fill on top of the larger fill. Set blend properties to a smooth blend (Choose Object ⇨ Blend ⇨ Blend Options and set the Spacing to Smooth). With the Blend tool, click an anchor at the bottom of the smaller, top drop, and click again on an anchor at the bottom of the larger, darker drop to generate a smooth blend between those two anchors.

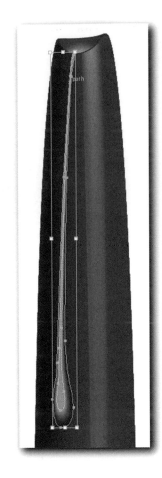

⑬ Drag the blended drop onto the candle.

ALTERNATIVE

Another (and simpler) approach to filling the large circle is to apply a radial gradient. The effect is different, but also works.

⑭ Assemble the candle, dropping wax and wick in place. Create a background for the wick by generating a smooth blend between a small yellow circle about the diameter of the wick, and a much larger blue circle.

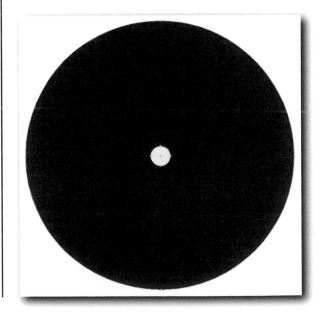

15 Move the blended yellow-to-blue circle behind the wick to generate a glow from the candle. Create a dark blue background for the whole illustration.

Generated Planet

It's surprisingly hard to find great vector global maps. The U.S. government and others make high-quality maps of the planet available, but they, of course, are bitmaps, not Illustrator-friendly vectors. Why not just work with a bitmapped map in Illustrator? One reason is that even 300 dpi maps look lousy when mapped onto a 3D effect. In order to produce a nicely mapped map, you need a vector file.

Tweaking and tuning a standardized vectorized map of the planet so that it applies with proper proportion to a globe is way too much work for anyone. The solution is to start with a Platte-Carrée projection map. You can convert raster Platte-Carrée maps to vectors, or buy Platte-Carrée vector maps in Illustrator format. I work with both in this project.

Commercially distributed vector maps, like those from the Map Resources web site, are highly complex. They include layers with detail that is great for many projects, but unnecessary and overkill for this one. And, as you've seen in previous 3D mapping projects, if you've tried them, artwork to be mapped should be kept *simple* in order to reduce the stress on your system resources and the file size of the completed project. The first phase of the task, then, is to strip down a map from Map Resources.

1 Open a file of a vectorized map in Illustrator.

2 To simplify the map for this project, hide all layers except for two or three.

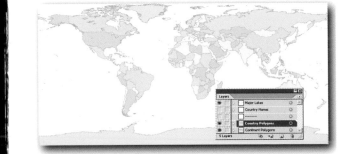

3 Continue reducing file size by flattening the layers (choose Flatten Artwork from the Layers palette fly-out menu.

> ## TIP
>
> The country and continent polygons provide a nice, simplified map.

> ## TIP
>
> There is no need, or good reason to maintain a link between the embedded JPEG and the file. You'll be messing with the JPEG, and will want to keep a clean version available.

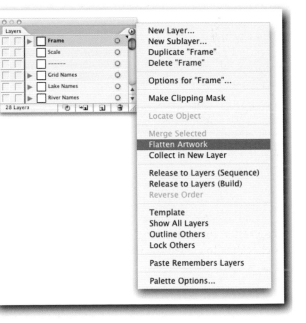

4 Finally, having reduced the size of the map, drag it into the Symbols palette and name it. If you develop a collection of mapped symbols, give them names that identify the projection.

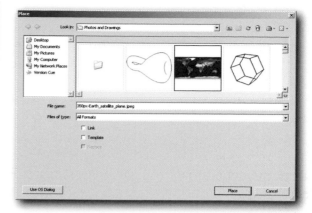

You can find Platte-Carrée format maps in Illustrator format for as little as $30 or so on the web (search for "Platte-Carrée Illustrator"). But for those of us for who can only dream of having $30, the low-budget alternative is to download a JPEG of a Platte-Carrée map, and trace it in Illustrator.

That didn't turn out to be as tough as I thought it might. All the people who sell Platte-Carrée maps provide free JPEGs as samples. Some of those maps trace quite well with Illustrator CS2's new Live Trace feature. NASA (the U.S. space agency) has some nice Earth photos in Platte-Carrée format as well that can be very cool.

To generate your own vectorized Platte-Carrée project globe, follow these steps:

(5) Download a JPEG Platte-Carrée projection map or photo.

(6) Create a new file in Illustrator. Choose File ➪ Place, and navigate to the downloaded JPEG (or other bitmap/raster format) in the Place dialog box. Clear the Link checkbox to embed the file in the Illustrator document and click Place.

TIP

The Color 16 preset of tracing parameters worked well with several of the JPEGs I converted to vector maps. But you can experiment with other presets, previewing each in the artboard before settling on a good fit for converting to vectors. You can tweak the tracing parameters if you really must by playing with the Threshold and Min Area sliders. The results preview in the artboard.

Platte-Carrée – the Key to Mapping the Planet

A Platte-Carrée map layout takes the latitude and longitude grids of our spherical planet, and distorts them onto a rectangle. Platte-Carrée maps look ridiculously distorted when laid out "flat" – like looking at yourself in a funhouse mirror. (Greenland and other land masses near the poles are stretched way out in length). But when you map a Platte-Carrée projection back onto a sphere, it loses the distortion and "fits."

The Platte Carrée (aka Equidistant Cylindrical Projection, aka Geographic Projection) layout has other uses, but in the modern era it's main claim to fame (and function) is the fact that it's mappable on 3D shapes.

You can easily find a raster Platte-Carrée world map on the web, but a vectorized format saves you the hassle of generating a vector file from a bitmap. Vectorized maps cost money, so this project has a version for folks who have resources to get a vectorized world map, and a low-budget version for those of us who need to save money by creating our own map from a traced bitmap.

Map Resources – www.mapresources.com – has hundreds of downloadable, royalty-free maps in Illustrator format. Each map file has many layers, so you can elect to display customized combinations of geographic features (mountains, rivers), political features (national borders), cities, and towns. The selection at Map Resources includes several Platte-Carrée maps.

Map Resources provides a free, sample downloadable vector map at its site. It isn't the same one used here, so your results may vary. But you can still have fun and master the techniques and produce a cool project for free.

You can find Platte-Carrée raster maps all over the Internet, some of them quite traceable. Look for ones without a lot of detail. NASA photos of earth are available in Platte-Carrée layout, and they work fine for this project. In this project, I use both a downloaded Illustrator map, and a converted raster image.

7 If the Control palette is not active, display it by selecting Window ⇨ Control Palette. With the placed bitmap selected, click the Live Trace button in the Control Panel to activate Live Trace mode.

8 From the Preset drop down in the Control Panel, choose the Color 16 preset.

9 Once you find the best settings to convert the map, click the Expand button to convert the bitmap to a vector. Use the Direct Selection tool to clean up extraneous paths.

10 Recolor the map as necessary.

11 Drag the new map into the Symbol palette to make it available for mapping. Give it a name, something like **Platte-Carrée Projection Earth**.

You can now delete the map itself; the version you need is in the Symbols palette and will be saved with the file.

The final phase is to place the Platte-Carrée projection on the revolved globe. Once you do, you can tilt the globe back and forth, or rotate it to any degree, and still see a proportional globe. With one or more mappable symbols of Platte-Carrée maps available, you're ready to generate the globe and place the map on it.

12 Prepare to generate a globe by drawing a semicircle. You can assign a fill color — like light blue. If you elect to apply shading at some point, the fill color will become useful. But apply *no* stroke.

13 With the semicircle selected, open the Effects dialog box by choosing Effect ⇨ 3D ⇨ Revolve. Set rotation to 180° for a complete rotation. From the Surface drop-down menu, choose No Shading. Hold off on other rotation settings for now. Don't click OK yet! You still have to map the map.

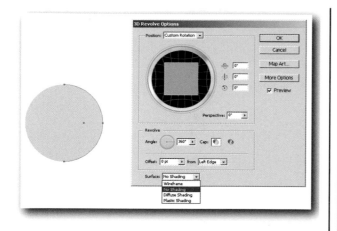

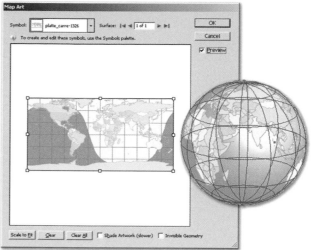

NOTE

If the map you use does not include oceans, you might want to adjust this step by assigning a blue fill to the revolved semicircle, and applying Plastic Shading. Use your creative judgment here.

14 Click the Map Art button to open the Map Art dialog box. The mappable surface is displayed.

15 Choose a map symbol from the Symbol drop-down list. Click the Preview button, if your system will bear that, and preview how the map appears on your globe.

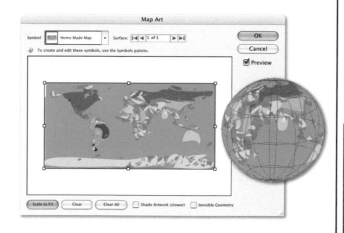

16 Click the Expand to Fill checkbox in the Map Options dialog box. Preview the state of your final project on the artboard.

17 Click OK to return to the 3D Revolve Options dialog box. Click the Preview checkbox if it is not selected, and interactively manipulate X, Y, and Z axes to display any perspective on our planet.

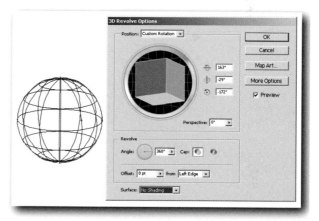

TIP

Because you are working from a revolved semicircle, there should be just one surface. Are you ending up with more surfaces? Make sure you have drawn a perfect semicircle — a good technique is selecting one anchor of a circle with the Direct Selection tool, and deleting it. Also, make sure you have no stroke assigned to the semicircle. In the weird and sometimes stupid logic of Illustrator surface generation, adding a stroke generates extra surfaces.

18 When you have picked a good angle on the planet, click OK in the 3D Revolve Options dialog box to generate a customized perspective on Earth.

The result here is a nice, rotatable globe. But wait! There's more. In the next task, you get to generate multiple rotations of the planet.

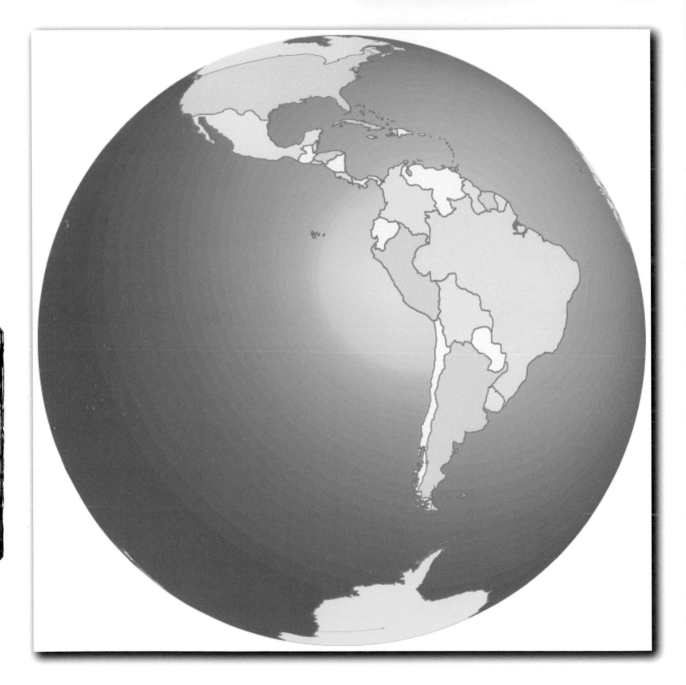

Revolving Planet Earth

In Task 7, I emphasize that anyone can find a raster image of Earth, but the advantage of mapping your own Earth is that you can custom rotate the planet. In this chapter, you multiply that effect by creating four rotating images to portray the rotation of the planet.

1 Start this project by opening the file you created in Task 7. Or, jump back there and create the mapped map of planet Earth.

2 Select the path of the globe generated in Task 7. In the Appearances palette, double-click the 3D Revolved Map row in the Appearance palette to open the 3D Revolve Options dialog box.

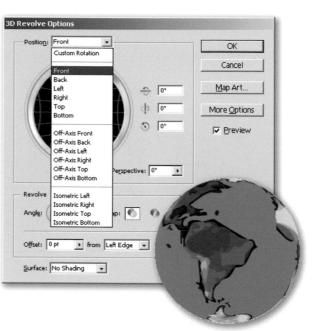

3 Set the X, Y, and Z boxes to 0 degrees. Why zero? You will be creating four versions of the globe, each rotated 25% (90 degrees). The math will be simpler if you start with a rotation of zero degrees. This is the same as the Front position preset available from the Position drop-down menu in the 3D Revolve Options dialog box. And, the next three positions are the same as the Right, Back, and Left presets, so rotation is easy. If your math skills are strong, and the perspective at 0 degrees sucks, feel free to start with another rotation angle around the Y (polar) axis.

CAUTION

The Paths generated from any effect aren't real — they are properties of the effect and cannot be edited in Illustrator without adjusting the effect. Most often, at the end of a 3D effect project, you will want to choose Object ➪ Expand Appearance to convert the effect into paths.

In other 3D effect projects, I've encouraged you to expand the effect into a real, editable set of Illustrator paths. For this project, however, you do *not* want to expand the effect. Instead, the resulting 3D image should remain an effect so you can take advantage of the fact that 3D effects can be modified.

4 Copy and paste the globe four times. Space the copies about a half-diameter of the globe apart.

5 Select all four globes. View the Align palette. Click the Vertical Align Center icon in the Align palette to align them on a horizontal plane.

6 Click the Horizontal Distribute Center icon in the Align palette to space the globes evenly.

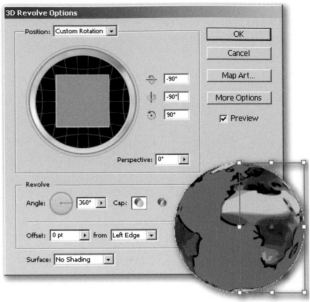

The next phase is rotating the copied globes 90 degrees each.

7 Select the second globe from the left. Double-click the 3D Revolve (Mapped) row in the Appearance palette to reopen the 3D Revolve Options dialog box.

8 Set the Position to 90 degrees Y-axis rotation by selecting Right from the Position preset drop-down menu.

9 Select the second globe from the left. Double-click the 3D Revolve (Mapped) row in the Appearance palette to reopen the 3D Revolve Options dialog box.

10 Set the Y-axis rotation to 180 degrees by selecting Back from the Position preset drop-down menu.

11 Select the third globe from the left. Double-click the 3D Revolve (Mapped) row in the Appearance palette to reopen the 3D Revolve Options dialog box.

(12) Set the Y-axis rotation to 270 degrees by selecting Left (same as –90 degrees) from the Position preset drop-down menu.

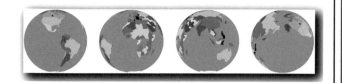

(13) Add times for each section of the revolving globe by looking up times at Time and Date (www.timeanddate.com/worldclock).

(14) Add a background, and arrange the rotating globes to display time in your favorite hangouts.

TIP

As you define 90-degree rotation for each globe, don't be afraid to tweak the X and Z rotation a bit. In reality, the Earth wobbles as it rotates. And you're going for an effect here anyway, not a detailed map.

EARTH TIME

La Paz
12 AM

Harare
6 AM

Taipai
12 NOON

Kiritmati
6 PM

chapter

2

fills and thrills

Fills need to get crazier. I hope this chapter contributes to that process.

Pattern fills can be designed from triangles, rectangles (not *just* squares), par-allelograms, pentagons, hexagons, and octagons. Because parallelograms are four-sided, and because hexagons and octagons are *essentially* triangles and rectangles, that leaves two main techniques for disrupting the dominant para-digm in pattern tiles: triangles and (non-square) rectangles.

Designing pattern fills from those two shapes will be the theme of the first two projects in this chapter. The flying monkeys, as you figured out already, are based on a triangle pattern. The "After the Big Bang" project uses a non-square rectangle as a pattern tile, and then adds another weird trick — but I won't spoil that for you.

Other fill provocations in this chapter include comic book pixelation, a flowable border design, and an excursion into gradient mesh territory.

Endless Iron Monkeys

In Woo-ping Yuen's amazing 1993 flick *Iron Monkey*, a corrupt and paranoid ruler suspects everyone of being the Robin Hood/Zorro–like "Iron Monkey." Even to the point of rounding up the real monkeys. In that spirit, this project creates a triad of monkeys that can be repeated in a provocative and non-stereotypical pattern. The essence of any tiling pattern is creating artwork that tiles properly. With squares, this means matching top, bottom, and sides. With a triangular pattern, it means designing an image around a pivot point, within an isosceles triangle frame.

TIP

Isosceles triangles have two sides with the same length, and therefore two equal triangles. Equilateral triangles are a subset of isosceles triangles—they have *three equal* sides (and angles). Equilateral triangles, as any good quilt-maker will tell you, are easiest to piece together into a tiling pattern.

The first step in designing a tiling, triangular pattern is to create an isometric grid full of equilateral triangles. There's a quick, cheap way to do this. It would be more precise to draw all the angled guides necessary, but I'm in a hurry, so here's the quick way:

① Find yourself a digital isometric grid pattern. You have three choices: 1) steal a piece of some kid's isometric grid paper and scan it; 2) buy your own isometric grid paper at an art supply store and scan it; or 3) find a raster file of an isometric grid on the web by searching for "isometric grid." Download it and save it.

② Import your isometric grid into a new Illustrator file by choosing File ➪ Place, navigating to the raster file, and placing it (don't link it).

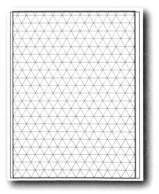

 With the placed raster grid selected, activate the Control palette (Window ➪ Control Palette). Because a raster object is selected, the Control palette includes the Live Trace button. The Technical Drawing preset in the Tracing Control palette should do a good job of identifying the grid pattern — choose that from the Preset popup in the Control palette, and then click the Live Trace button.

④ Click Expand in the Control palette to convert the raster isometric grid to vectors.

⑤ Before converting the vector grid to guides, rescale your grid if necessary so you have decently large equilateral triangles.

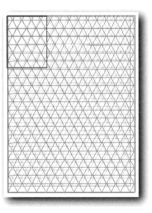

TIP

Rescale the grid while maintaining the aspect ratio of the equilateral triangles by holding down the Shift key while rescaling the grouped grid.

6 Clean up stray points or lines that should not be part of the grid.

7 With the whole grid selected, choose View ➪ Guides ➪ Make Guides.

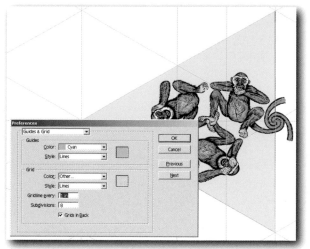

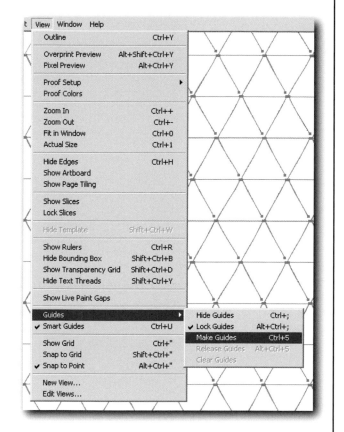

* Use horizontal and vertical grids to align elements of your drawing within the equilateral triangle.

* Constrain the repeating pattern itself inside an equilateral triangle, as defined by the isosceles guides you generated.

* An essential trick: Create a pivotable element in the illustration. Here, it is the monkeys' tails. Note that only one monkey has . . . three tails. When the illustration is rotated 60 degrees, the tails will match. (Again, use some trial and error.)

Drawing a triangular design that repeats around a pivot point takes . . . I was going to say *monkeying* around, but I'll say trial and error instead. I can't really provide step-by-step instructions for the drawing (it was originally sketched, then scanned, traced, and touched up in Illustrator). But here are some tips:

* Display horizontal and vertical guides as well as the isometric grid you converted to guides earlier in this project. Set grid settings by choosing Illustrator/ Edit ➪ Preferences ➪ Guides & Grid. Choose a wide grid increment in the Gridline Every box — something like an inch.

NOTE

For a simple triangular rotation project, you might draw a single leaf, with a stem that ends at what will become a pivot point.

8 Illustrator doesn't offer any tricks such as swatch patterns for rotating isometric patterns. Instead, you need to group your drawing and then copy/rotate it. You use Illustrator's Rotate tool, and the special feature that allows you to rotate around a selected anchor — which in this case is the pivot point around which your illustration will rotate. Start by deleting any elements of the drawing you don't want rotated, or that you created to help align objects within the drawing.

9 With the Pen tool, define an anchor on the pivot point around which the illustration will rotate.

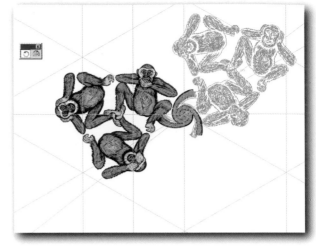

10 Select Illustrator/Edit ➪ Preferences ➪ Smart Guides & Slides, and set the Angles popup to 60 degrees. Group everything and select the grouped objects. Select the Rotate tool, and click the anchor point you defined as the rotation point. Hold down the Option/Alt key to duplicate while rotating, and hold down the Shift key to snap to rotation angles. With your fingers thus engaged, click and drag on another anchor in the illustration, and rotate 120 degrees clockwise.

NOTE

You can use any shape as a clipping mask.

11 Repeat Step 10, but this time drag counterclockwise to create the third element of the triangular repeating pattern.

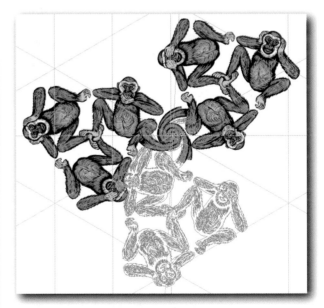

Because this tiling pattern involves simple copy and pasting, essentially, you can tweak the pattern to make elements match after rotating and duplicating. Once you have a touched-up triad pattern of three rotated triangles, group *those* three triangles, and start the process again.

12 Because your final pattern will not fit into a rectangle (it is, after all, a bunch of triangles), the finishing touch is to create a rectangular clipping mask — assuming your final pattern is to fit into a rectangle. Apply the clipping mask by selecting both the underlying illustration and the clipping rectangle, and choose Object ➪ Clipping Mask ➪ Make.

The final result is a unique, interesting pattern that breaks the mold of rectangular fills.

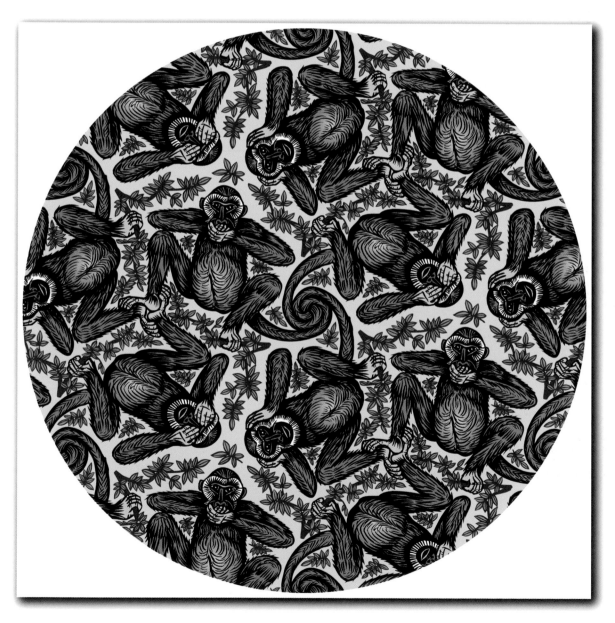

After the Big Bang

In this project, you create a flexible pattern fill that can be applied to any shape. The first phase is creating a star field background. The second phase is cropping the star field so it tiles neatly. What we call stars took billions of years to evolve, but to save time, you generate some in Illustrator in a few minutes. Even though Illustrator has a Star tool, I recommend creating more realistic and spacey stars by enhancing the generated stars with some puckering. Final touching up is done by editing selected anchors in the star, and filling it with a gradient.

1 Select the Star tool and click on the artboard to activate the Star dialog box. Define a star with 5 points, about a .5-inch outside radius, and about a .25-inch inside radius.

2 Duplicate the star. Rotate the second star about 30 degrees. With the second star selected, choose Effect ⇨ Distort & Transform ⇨ Pucker & Bloat to open the Pucker and Bloat palette. Apply a Pucker of about 50%.

3 Tweak the puckered star by selecting the inside anchors with the Direct Selection tool, and double-clicking the Scale tool to open the Scale palette. Scale the inside anchors to about 50%.

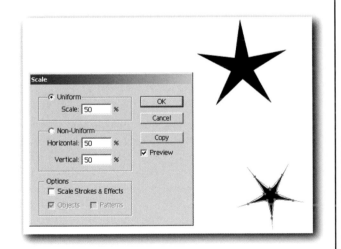

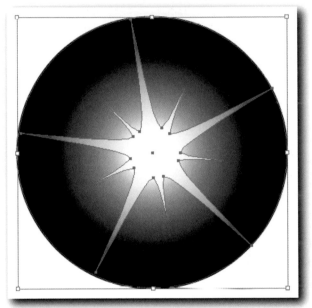

4 Apply a 25% pucker to the original star. Then, draw a circle with the diameter of the larger star. Apply a radial black-to-white fill to the circle and both stars. Center-align all three objects, with the circle behind the stars.

5 Group the stars and circle. Then, hold onto that star! You'll be duplicating it soon to populate the cosmos. Start drawing your comet by transforming a curved line into a path and filling it with a gradient to make the tale. Add circles to create what would be a sperm cell in another kind of illustration, but in this project will serve as a comet. Then, draw a curve using whatever technique you're most comfortable with. The Pen tool, the unprestigious Pencil tool, or just the Arc tool.

6 Use the Stroke palette to assign a 4-point weight to the stroke. Choose Object ⇨ Path ⇨ Outline Stroke to convert the (selected) curve to an outline. Use the Delete Anchor Point tool, the Convert Anchor Point tool, and the Direct Selection tool to edit the path to create a comet shape. Apply a linear black-to-white gradient fill, and adjust the gradient angle in the Gradient palette so most of the tail of the comet is dark, while the wider end is lighter.

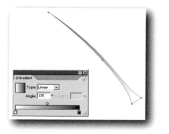

7 Create the comet "head" by drawing two circles, one about .12 inch diameter, one about .18 inch diameter. Apply a black-to-white radial gradient to both, and center the smaller one on top of the larger one. For the radial gradient fill in both circles, set the location to about 75% for logarithmically increasing dark shading.

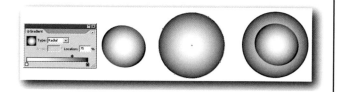

8 You guessed what comes next: Pin the tail on the comet. As you do this, arrange the *smaller* circle in front of the comet tail and the larger one behind the tale. You can preview how the comet will look when released into outer space by placing it against a black background.

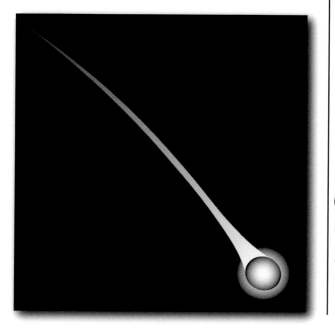

9 In preparation for generating a tile, draw a 2.5-inch black square. Assign a colored stroke for now — a temporary thing that will be helpful in creating the tile pattern later. Copy, rotate, and scale the star and comet to fill the tile with stars and comets. For now, *do not* have any of the objects extend beyond the edge of the tile.

With the basic tiling pattern designed, duplicate the tile to get a sense of how it will look as a fill. Then, push the envelope by extending comet tails across tile borders, and "re-cutting" a tile that appears to have a comet shooting out of, and back into it.

In patterning the tile, instead of a square tile, you create a half-drop repeat. This is a design technique frequently used for textile pattern design. Half-drop repeats are more interesting and less "boxy" than simpler side-to-side repeats, and create a much more seamless, "patternless"-looking pattern.

Here's how that's done:

10 Group the whole pattern. You copy and paste it in the remaining steps. Copy and paste the rectangle and star contents and align three of the tiles vertically. Paste two copies of the tile on each side (you want a total of seven tiles). Align the side tiles so the line where they meet vertically aligns with the center of the original tile.

TIP

To make objects easier to align, it's sometimes helpful to use the Attributes panel, and (with any object selected) click the Show Center button to identify the center of the object. This makes for easier vertical or horizontal center alignment using Guides.

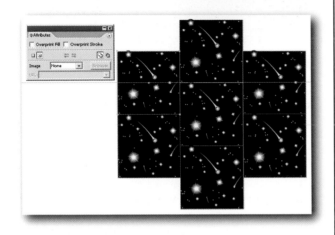

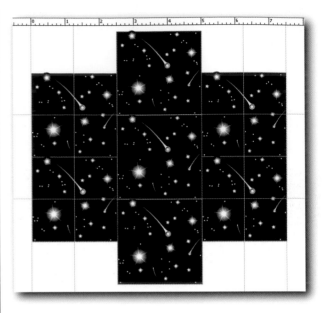

11) To prepare to "cut a tile" that does not appear to be tiled, adjust the stars to make a pleasing layout by selecting the same stars in each current tile and moving them together.

NOTE

The idea here is to avoid large gaps or star positions that create visual lines. Have some of the stars *cross* the rectangle borders so there will be no empty "lanes" in the repeating starfield that is produced when this rectangle is tiled.

12) Use Guides that intersect to define the area that will be the final tile. The Guides should be 5 inches apart horizontally (twice the width of the original tile, and running from the middle of the left tile to the middle of the right tile). The vertical guides should match the top and bottom of the original tile.

13) Satisfied that your layout pushes the limits of space far enough? I'm not. Step back and re-look at your tile design. Select *all* your large comets and move them together so that some of them cross out of the area you have now defined as the future rectangular tile. This has to be done with *all* of similar (in this case comets) objects selected to maintain the integrity of the tile.

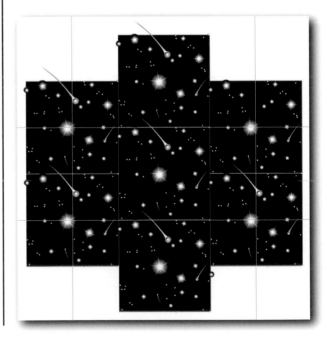

Essentially, all that's left to create a pattern fill swatch is to trim it to its essential elements and drag it into the Swatch palette.

(14) First, do basic cleanup by deleting all the original black rectangles. Then, draw a new black rectangle the size of the rectangle formed by the Guides. Delete all the objects *outside* the object that don't overlap the new black rectangle.

TIP

You'll find it easier to select and delete all the objects that don't overlap the rectangle by jumping to outline view (Command/Ctrl+Y) to see and delete all that junk. Use Command/Ctrl+Y again to toggle back to Preview view.

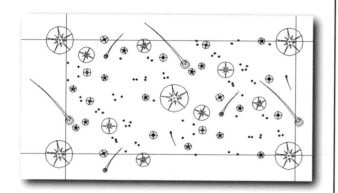

(15) Copy the rectangle into the clipboard. Press Command/Ctrl+B to paste the rectangle to the back of all the objects. Remove any fill or stroke from the rectangle. Select all the objects that are part of the pattern, and drag them all into the Swatches palette. Double-click the newly created swatch, and name it **Space Background**.

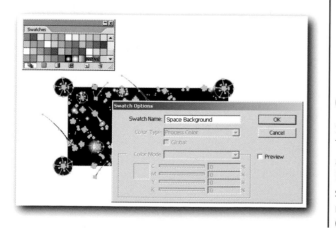

(16) Try out your fill. The swatch is ready to apply as a fill to *any* shape.

(17) You can share this swatch with other Illustrator files. You don't have to open a file to access the swatch. To access a swatch palette from another file, choose Window ➪ Swatch Libraries ➪ Other Library. The Select a Library to Open dialog box opens. Navigate to the (Illustrator) file that has the swatch palette you wish to access. Select that file and click Open. The Swatch Library from the selected file opens and is accessible as a palette in your current project. You can then apply the swatch you created to *any* path or illustration.

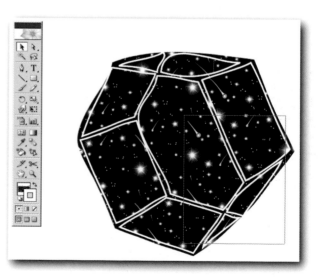

(18) You can also adjust the way a swatch pattern displays as a fill by dragging on the fill with the Selection tool, while holding down the Tilde (~) key. Tragically, there is no interactive preview for this feature, and it looks — as you adjust the fill — like you are just moving the object. In fact, it looks so much like moving the selected object that if you forget to hold down the (not really the) Tilde key, you *will* move the object. You just press Command/Ctrl+Z to undo misfires, and try again.

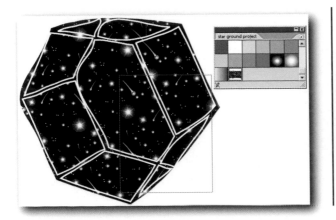

Pondering the Shape of the Universe?

For discussion, and diagrams and illustrations reflecting perspectives on the shape of the universe, see www.geom. uiuc.edu/~teach95/sos95/big-picture.

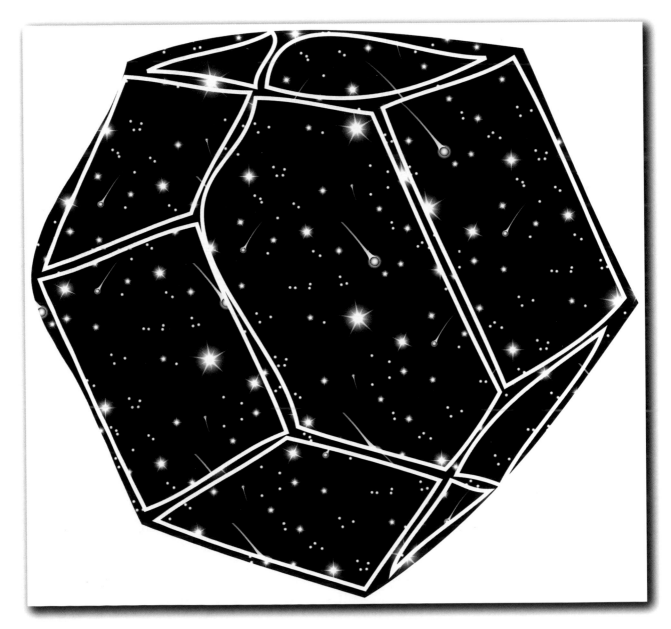

Comic Book Pixelation

In this project, you apply Lichtenstein-like fills to comic illustrations. I never really appreciated Roy Liechtenstein before I saw the huge retrospective of his that toured the U.S. in 2004. Everyone has seen his enlarged, exaggerated comic book panels, but he also applied his minimalist deconstruction attack to a wide variety of illustrations. For an interesting perspective on the comic art side of Lichtenstein, visit http://davidbarsalou.homestead.com/LICHTENSTEINPROJECT.html.

The two substantially new features of Ilustrator CS2, Live Tracing and Live Paint, are custom made for importing scanned comic drawings and applying fills to them. You'll see in this project. All you need is a comic book drawing. If you don't have one, run out and pick up a comic book and scan a panel. I'll wait . . . Back? Okay, then, let's go.

1. Scan in the source artwork as a TIFF file using the Black-and-White or Ink Drawing profile in your scanner software. Once you've scanned your illustration to a TIFF file, you're ready to place it in an Illustrator file.

2. With a new Illustrator file open, choose File ⇨ Place, and navigate in the Place dialog box to find your scanned artwork. Don't select the Link checkbox. You don't want or need to link the editing you do on the original to the illustration you are generating.

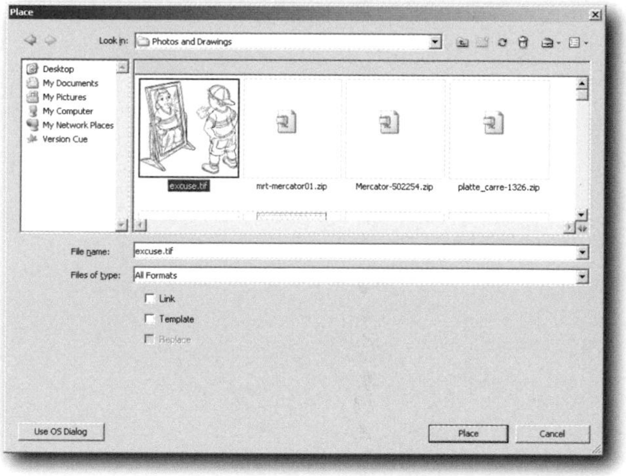

3. With the scanned TIFF image placed in an Illustrator file, activate the Control palette (Window ⇨ Control Palette). Because a raster object is selected, the Control palette includes the Live Trace button.

4. Click the Live Trace button. The Comic Art preset in the Tracing Control palette was designed just for importing and converting comic drawings.

5. Preview the Live Trace results: The most efficient way to preview Live Trace results is to choose No Image from the Preview Different Views of the Raster Image fly-out menu on the Control palette, and to choose Tracing Result from the Preview Different Views of the Vector Result fly-out.

6. Click Live Paint in the Control palette to convert the raster comic artwork to special Live Paint regions that can have fills applied easily.

The Logic of Live Paint Groups

In Illustrator, intersecting lines hardly affect each other. Like cars passing over each other on a freeway overpass, intersecting lines don't *cut* each other, they just fly over each other.

Illustrator veterans know that they can count on a stroke being a stroke. From beginning to end, it has unified properties. Closed paths are closed paths, and like strokes, they can be laid on top of each other, but they don't *cut into* each other.

In order to create new paths from intersecting strokes, it has been necessary to use the Pathfinder tools. Live Paint regions are *kind of* like areas where the Pathfinder Divide tool has been applied. Intersecting lines generate new paths. And most significantly, regions formed by contiguous intersecting lines become editable fill areas.

In general, you want to work with Live Paint groups when you want to easily assign fills to anything that *looks* like a path, and you want to *expand* Live Paint regions when you want to edit paths.

When you design the fill patterns, don't worry about final scaling, except for the *relative* scale of your dot pattern to the enclosing square. Working on the tiny scale needed to create dot pattern fills is tedious and unnecessary. Instead, you rescale the fill patterns after you apply them.

NOTE

If your Live Trace didn't work well, experiment with other presets. If none of the presets are creating a Live Trace result that is workable, you can create your own settings by clicking the Tracing Options dialog box icon in the Live Trace Control palette. The Tracing Options dialog box lets you change color modes, gap settings, and other details. And, it's interactive — so you can fool around with trace settings and preview the results on the artboard.

If you *still* don't get a decent trace result, dont' click the Live Paint button to generate Live Paint regions directly from the tracing process. Instead, click Expand in the Live Trace Control palette. Use Illustrator editing techniques to clean up the vectors. Then, select everything and choose object ⇨ Live Paint ⇨ Make from the menu.

(7) Draw a square about .25" wide and high.

(8) Fill it with a visible color for now, and zoom in (press Z to activate the Zoom tool and draw a marquee around the square). Draw a circle about .2" in diameter. Place it inside the square. Apply a bright yellow fill to the circle. Change the fill of the square to white.

(9) With both the square and the circle selected, view the Align palette (Shift+F7 toggles between displaying and hiding the Align palette). Click the Vertical Align Center icon in the Align palette. Click the Horizontal Align Center icon in the Align palette.

(10) Before converting the pattern into a swatch, make a bunch of copies and alter the fill color of the circle so you have more options for dot fills. Experiment with a black stroke color on a few of your copies.

NOTE

If necessary, Command/right-click on the rectangle and choose Arrange ⇨ Send to Back from the Context menu so that the square is *behind* the circle.

(11) Turn each square/circle combination into a Pattern fill tile by dragging them (grouped) into the Swatch palette. The basic concept behind the dot pattern fill you are creating is that you're placing a colored dot (circle) inside a white square just large enough to define the spacing in the illustration. You can use the two types of comic book fills along with solid colors (or gradients) to complete comic book panels.

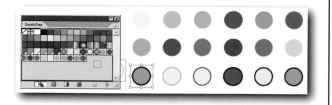

(12) If you expanded your artwork, instead of generating a Live Paint group when you converted it from vectors, or if you drew your artwork in Illustrator, you need to convert the paths to a Live Paint region. Select the entire comic book panel you imported and traced. Click the Live Paint Bucket tool in the Toolbox (or press K). Click on the selected paths in your artwork. The enclosed areas are converted to a Live Paint group.

(13) Load the Live Paint Bucket tool with a color swatch by clicking the Fill icon in the Tools palette, and clicking on a color Swatch. The selected swatch displays in the Toolbox.

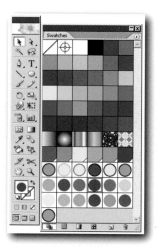

(14) Click the Live Paint Bucket tool (K), and click on one of the generated Live Paint regions in the Live Paint

group you created. The selected region displays a disorienting wide red outline.

15 Click outside the selected Live Paint region to see the effect of the fill. Repeat the process, filling in your illustration with a combination of pattern and solid color fills.

16 The Scale tool can be used to rescale objects, fills, or both. Here, you just want to rescale the fill patterns. Rescaling fill patterns requires you to enter into the weird and semi-charted world of how Live Paint regions are managed. You cannot select a Live Paint region and reliably edit

TIP

The Live Paint Bucket tool works fine with any swatch, including color swatches. You don't have to just use swatches you created. The Skintones Swatch palette is especially useful for assigning a multi-racial array of skin color fills.

You'll find it much easier to apply the Live Paint tool if you zoom in several times on an element of your illustration. As you hover over Live Paint regions, the Brush icon indicates a selected stroke, and the Paint Bucket icon indicates you have selected a Live Paint fill region.

the Fill Pattern scaling. But you can select paths the old-fashioned way, and tweak fill pattern scaling. So, you'll now forget about Live Paint, and use regular selection tools. Select your entire illustration. You'll apply scaling to all pattern fills within the illustration.

17 With your entire illustration, or part of it with dot fill patterns selected, double-click the Scale tool. In the Options area of the Scale dialog box, deselect all options *except* Patterns. (The Patterns checkbox *should* be selected.) To enlarge the dot pattern, enter a percentage over 100 in the Uniform Scale area. To condense the dot pattern, enter a percentage less than 100 in the Uniform Scale area

NOTE

If you want to apply different scaling options to different fill patterns within your illustration, you need to expand the appearance of the Live Paint areas. Do that by clicking the Expand button in the Live Paint Options palette with the Live Paint group selected.

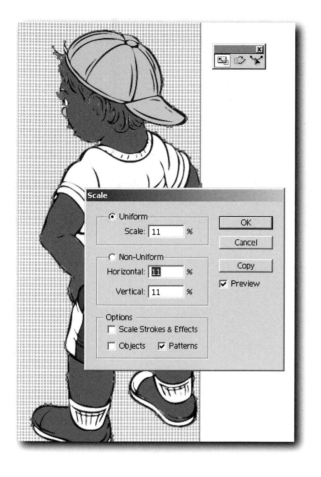

18 Finish off your comic illustration by touching up colors and applying dot patterns and other fills.

NOTE

If your dot patterns display as gridlines on screen when you generate small, condensed dot patterns, those gridlines are visual artifacts. They are a product of your monitor's inability to correctly display high-resolution dot patterns.

They don't show up in printed results. On the other hand, if you're preparing your work for digital or web display, you might want to avoid very small dot patterns that appear as grids in some viewing environments.

Tribal Borders

Distinctive borders can turn a blah illustration into an interesting one. If you're looking for inspiration for border patterns, check out Co Spinhoven's *Celtic Stencil Designs, Arabic Art in Color* edited by Prisse D'Avennes, *Designs and Patterns From Historic Ornament* by W. and G. Audsley, or *Art Deco Designs in Color* edited by Charles Rahn Fry.

This particular border pattern requires some skill with the Pen tool. Find yourself a border pattern that fits your Pen skill level, and adapt these steps accordingly.

1 As with many complex (or even simple, but sophisticated) Illustrator projects, a key element is defining a useful grid and necessary guides. In this case, you define a tight grid, turn on snap to grid, and create a 45-degree angle guide. Define a grid with ¹/₁₆-inch increments by choosing Illustrator/Edit ➪ Preferences ➪ Guides and Grid. Set the Gridline Every box to .06 inches. (If you type in ¹/₁₆, Illustrator does the math for you.)

2 Click OK. Choose View ➪ Show Grid. Choose View ➪ Snap to Grid to facilitate aligning the elements of the border.

3 View rulers (Command/Ctrl+R toggles them on and off). Drag the horizontal (top) ruler down onto the artboard.

4 Choose View ➪ Guides and deselect Lock Guides so the guide can be edited.

5 Select the guide with the Direct Selection tool. Double-lick the Rotate tool, and enter 45 degrees. Click the Preview checkbox to see the result. Click OK. With this grid setup, it is possible to draw the elements of the border.

6 Availing yourself of the grid and the 45-degree guide, draw a border, about an inch wide, with a 9-point stroke. You can reduce the scale or width later, but anything narrower will be difficult to draw.

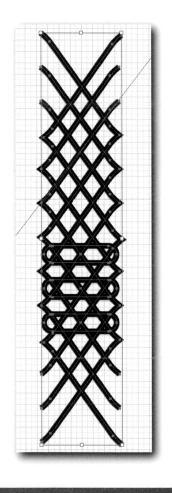

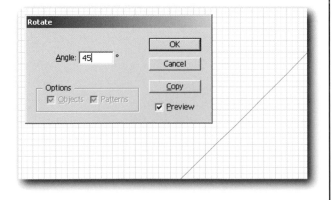

TIP

For this border, draw the zig-zagging 45-degree angle lines first. Add the rounded rectangles later.

7 Rotate and copy the border to create a horizontal edge.

8 Draw the corner segment.

9 Draw a center element that will be used to break up the top, bottom, and side borders. Whether you duplicated the pattern here or not, if you have a top/bottom segment, a side segment, and a corner segment, you have enough elements to put them together into a border.

10 Strokes can't have fills, but outlined strokes can. Finishing the frame involves converting the strokes to outlines, assigning fill and stroke color, and lining everything up. Select all the elements of your border (you might make a safe copy first), and choose Object ⇨ Path ⇨ Outline Stroke.

11 Apply a fill and stroke color to the new paths.

12 Align the corner element with the sides. If you created middle elements as well, place them.

13 Copy and rotate the one corner to create the additional three corners. Repeat the side and top/bottom segments as necessary to complete the frame.

Mask in a Mesh

Gradient mesh fills are great for highly stylized illustrations. The publisher of one of my recent books insisted on a gradient mesh illustration for the book cover, to get a jump-off-the-page, 3D textured look. In this project, you draw a simple mask, with only a few closed paths. Most of these paths will become gradient mesh areas. The *mesh* comes from the fact that gradient mesh fills have an underlying *grid* (or mesh). Every intersecting line in the grid is editable — in location, and in color. There are a number of techniques for generating a gradient mesh, but the most useful is to create the *basic* outline of your illustration first, and then apply a gradient mesh to that outline.

 Draw a simple mask. Use your favorite horror or comic character, or make something up. Keep the illustration *simple!* No fill is necessary at this point. And don't worry about details in the outline; that will be adjusted with the gradient mesh.

2 Select the path that will be the mouth for the mask (if your illustration is grouped, use the Direct Selection tool).

3 Apply a fill color to the mouth that is close to the mesh colors you will be generating. Apply no stroke.

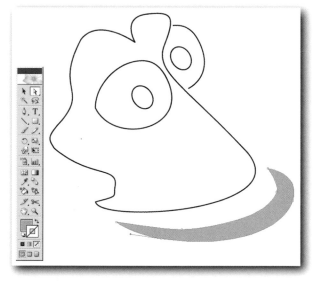

4 With *just* the mouth selected (rely on the Group Selection tool), choose Object ⇨ Create Gradient Mesh. The Gradient Mesh dialog box appears. Click the Preview checkbox to interactively adjust gradient mesh settings.

5 Because the mouth is long and thin, you want more columns than rows. Define five columns, and two rows. Set the Appearance to Edge, and leave Highlight at 100%.

NOTE

Gradient mesh objects do not have stroke color. If you need a stroke around a gradient mesh, you need to create a duplicate of the object before applying the gradient mesh, and apply a stroke color to that copy. Then place the outline on top of the gradient mesh at the end of the process.

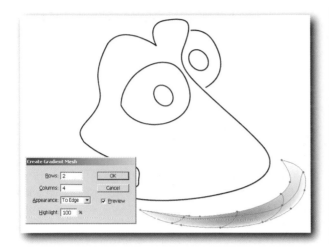

TIP

Even with Smart Guides, it is often very difficult to identify and select gradient mesh anchors. When you need
more help, switch to Outline view. Then toggle back to
Preview view to adjust gradient mesh point colors.

6 Select the main part of the mask. Apply a fill color
close to the one you want to end up with. Apply no
stroke. For this larger path, you want more flexibility in
defining the gradient mesh, so create four columns and four
rows. Set the Appearance to Center, and Highlight to 100%.

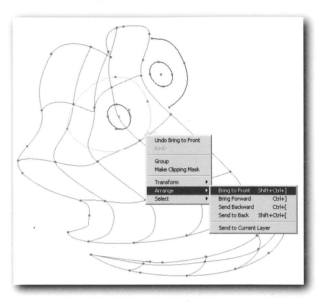

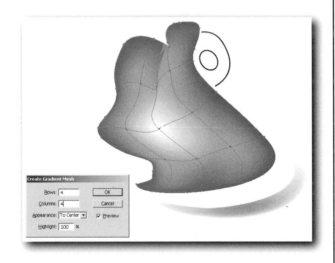

8 Not all elements need gradient mesh fills! Apply regular fills and strokes to eyes.

7 Use Command/Ctrl+Y to bounce back and forth
between Outline and Preview views. As you apply gradient meshes to objects, they might cover up other objects.
Later, you rely on Outline view to find hard-to-detect
gradient mesh anchors and control points. Use the Context
menu to move selected paths to the front as necessary.

chapter 2 ● fills and thrills

9 Edit the gradient mesh on the face first. Gradient mesh anchor points have control points, just like regular anchor points do. Use the Direct Selection tool to select anchor points on the outside of the gradient mesh. Drag them with the Direct selection tool to alter the outside shape of the face.

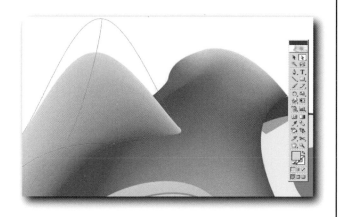

10 Use the anchor control points to tune the curve of the gradient mesh anchors, just as you would adjust the control points on a normal anchor.

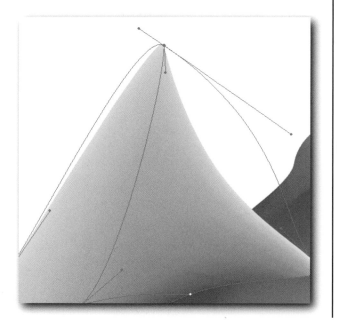

11 Continue to adjust the location and curve of all the gradient mesh anchors and control points on the outside of the gradient mesh to fine-tune the shape of the face.

12 Gradient mesh anchors on the outside of the mesh define the shape of the gradient mesh object. They also affect the color blending. Adjust the gradient mesh anchors on the outside of other elements of the illustration — such as the mouth.

13 Gradient mesh anchors *inside* the outline just affect the color blends. Select and move internal gradient mesh anchors. You can locate anchors (and paths) by hovering over the gradient mesh with Smart Guides on (Command/Ctrl+U toggles Smart Guides on and off).

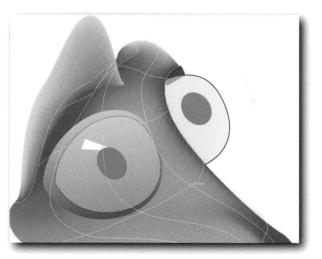

14 Apply a color from a color palette to the selected anchor. Moving an internal anchor does not change the shape of the gradient mesh, but it does affect the location of color gradient "hot spots" from which colors flow. Similarly, while internal gradient mesh anchor control points do not change the shape of the outside of the mesh, they do control the "flow" of color gradients radiating from that anchor. Adjust control point handles to control the flow of the color you assign to the gradient mesh anchor. Continue tweaking gradient mesh anchor colors, locations, and control point handles to fine-tune the appearance of your mask. Add other objects with regular fills to finish the mask.

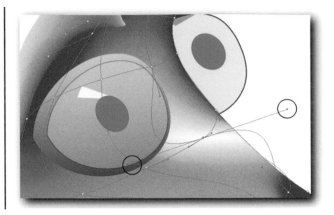

bent out of shapes

Some of the craziest things you can do in Illustrator happen by simply manipulating shapes in ways that disrupt typical visual patterns and processes. The projects in this chapter start with simple rectangles and ovals, and explore a bit of the infinite set of ways those two basic shapes can interact, morph into each other, and contrast with each other.

The first three projects in this chapter – Escher's Morphs, Escher Warps, and Escher Escapes – are pulled out of a social commentary Bruce K. Hopkins did several years ago called Cube Man. That project, in turn, reflects some of the really pathbreaking work done by the amazing M. C. Escher. In the last two projects in this chapter – "Stolen Jewels" and "Band of Gold" – I show you how simply stacking, rotating, and applying Live Paint grouping to shapes can create a jewel from humble hexagons and ellipses.

Escher Morphs

In this task, you take advantage of Illustrator CS2's ability to easily set up a perspective grid with angled Guides. With angled, perspective Guides in place, it's easy to morph squares toward another dimension.

The Jefferson Airplane, riffing off Lewis Carroll's *Alice in Wonderland*, sang about "when the men on the chessboard get up and tell you where to go." In this first of three connected projects, the squares on a chessboard-like grid begin their journey off of the chessboard and into three dimensions.

Real chessboards are 8 × 8. The one you use for this illustration has ten rows instead of eight. The squares are one-quarter inch . You create the "chessboard" by drawing intersecting lines, tic-tac-toe style, and then break them into paintable squares using Live Paint.

(1) Define grid spacing at ¼ inch. Do this by choosing Illustrator/Edit ➪ Preferences ➪ Guides & Grid. In the Grids Every box, let Illustrator perform the math — just enter **1/4 in**. Illustrator converts to the decimal (.25 inches).

(2) Using the Line tool, draw grid 8 squares wide, and ten squares high. Space rows and columns using the ¼-inch grids you defined.

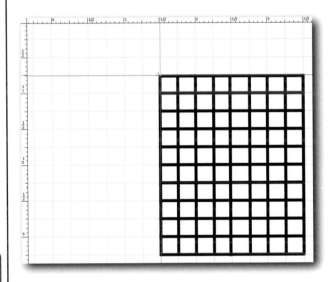

TIP

To make it easy to keep track of rows and columns, reset the grids to 0 at the top-left corner of your chessboard by viewing rulers, and dragging the upper-left corner of the rulers (where the horizontal and vertical rulers intersect) to the spot on the artboard that will be the top-left corner of your "chessboard." Turn on Snap to Grid (Shift+Command/Ctrl+").

When you draw the grid, precision is not important. As this project develops, you'll be warping the squares anyway, so don't obsess over aligning them perfectly.

(3) Select the entire chessboard, and click Option/Alt+Command/Ctrl+X to convert the grid into a Live Paint group. Press K to select the Live Paint tool, and paint the left column black.

(4) Fill in the rest of the squares as shown. Change the stroke display for the entire grid to no stroke.

5 Add the cube person's face.

6 Copy the chessboard. The second chessboard morphs.

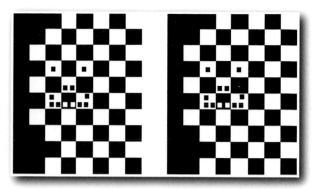

You create six angled Guides to provide the perspective and lines for beginning to warp the squares into 3D cubes. The basic technique for creating each of these Guides is the same, but the location and angles of the Guides are different.

7 Reset the rulers so the top-left corner of the *second* (copy) chessboard is at 0, 0.

8 Unlock Guides (Option/Alt+Command/Ctrl+;).

NOTE

You use the remaining steps to create six different perspective grid guides. The settings for the first perspective Guide are in the following steps. The specs for the remaining Guides are illustrated and listed at the end of this set of steps.

9 Create a new Guide (by pulling down from the horizontal or vertical ruler). Align the first horizontal Guide with the top of the chessboard.

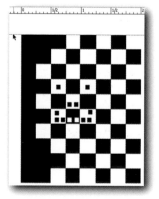

10 View the Info palette (F8 function key toggles display). You need this to set angles for the Guides.

11 With the Guide selected and aligned, click R to activate the Rotate tool. Click once on the Guide at the top of the upper-left corner of the upper-left square on the chessboard.

NOTE

The Guide you select, and where you click on the Guide, will be different for each Guide. Details for the other five Guides are at the end of these steps.

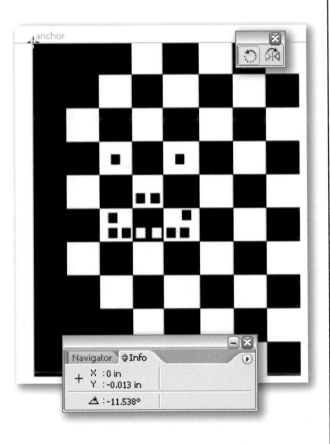

NOTE

View the rotation angle in the Info palette. These angle settings do *not* have to be exact. If you come within a degree, or two, or three, the project will work fine.

12 Use the Selection tool to rotate the Guide to about −12 degrees.

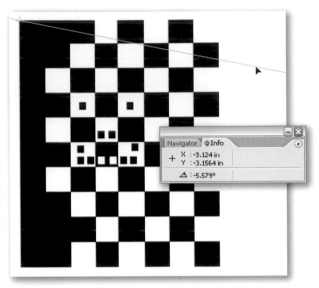

13 Create additional Guides:

* Starting at the upper-left corner of the second square in the first column: 15 degrees

* Starting at the upper-left corner of the third square in the first column: 15 degrees

* Starting at the upper-left corner of the seventh square in the first column: −35 degrees

* Starting at the upper-left corner of the tenth (last) square in the first column: 25 degrees

* Starting at the lower-left corner of the sixth square in the tenth (last) row: 35 degrees

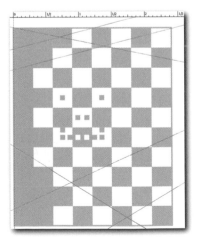

With your angled grid lines in place, you have Guides to help the squares evolve perspective.

Leave the original "chessboard" alone as you complete the project. It will stand as a contrast to the warped version you create as its evolved cousin.

Working only on the second chessboard, you use the perspective guides as a *general* orientation for drawing parallelograms and triangles to replace most of the squares in the grid. Lock your Guides (use Option/Alt+Command/Ctrl+; to toggle them locked), and get out your Pen tool.

(14) Delete all the black squares in the second chessboard except for the left column, and the black square in the third column of the top row.

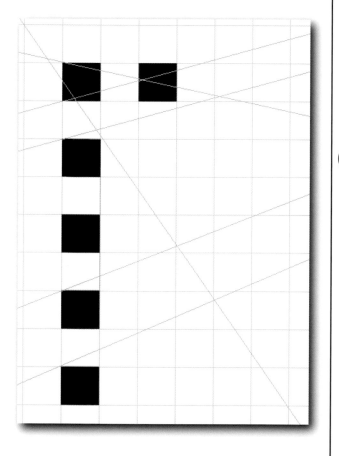

TIP

As necessary, unlock, move, and copy the Guides to help align the diamonds. You might make several copies of the –12-degree Guide you created in the previous section of this task to assist in creating the diamonds you need for this section of the illustration.

(15) Using the Guides for help with perspective, redraw the face, converting the rectangles to diamonds.

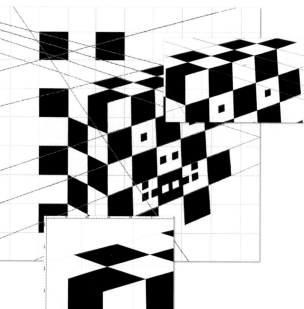

(16) Add a row of ten triangles in the last column.

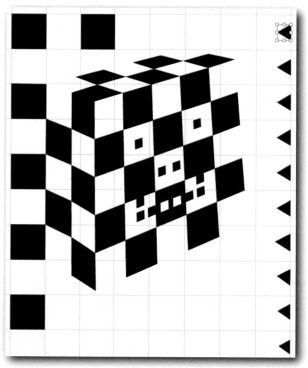

19 For the final touch, add a bunch of smaller diamonds on the upper-left corner of what is no longer much of a chessboard.

20 *Save this file* — you use it in the following tasks. For convenience, call it **grid.ai**.

Escher Warps

In this intermediate phase of this set of three tasks, you finish the evolution of a chessboard into a 3D cube background. Building on that background, you start getting really Escherish by having new cubes bust out of the backdrop.

WARNING

If you haven't created the file grid.ai in Task 14, do that before moving onto this phase. If you have created that file, open it. You add the work in this task to the overall project.

TIP

Three-tenths of an inch is an odd dimension to work with on a ruler. You might Ctrl/right-click on the vertical ruler and convert to millimeters (using the Context menu) for this particular measurement, and then flip back to inches to continue using the ruler.

① Create a 30-degree Guide to help with the perspective issues in this task. To quickly define a 30-degree Guide:

* Create a new horizontal Guide (pulled down from the top ruler).

* If the Guides are locked, press Option/Alt+Command/Ctrl+; to toggle them to an unlocked state.

* With the Guide selected, double-click the Rotate tool.

* Enter **30** in the Angle box and click OK in the Rotate dialog box.

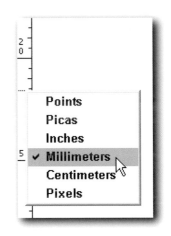

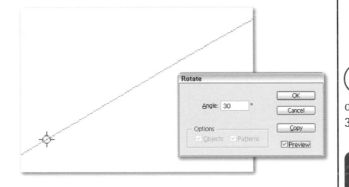

② Create a horizontal Guide as well to help align perspectives. Duplicate the horizontal Guide, and using the vertical ruler, place it about .3 inches below the first Guide.

③ Availing yourself of the 30-degree Guide, and the two horizontal Guides you created, draw a parallelogram with a vertical dimension of about .3 inches, and a 30-degree angled horizontal length of about .45 inches.

NOTE

You want a consistent stroke for all the paths in this and the related tasks. A setting of 2 points will work fine.

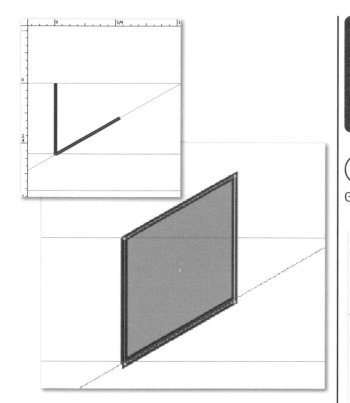

⑤ Complete the cube by drawing the top piece. Use your 30-degree Guide, and create a new –30 degree Guide to assist in drawing the angles.

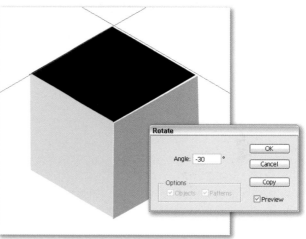

④ With the parallelogram selected, double-click the Reflect tool and Copy and Vertical reflect the selected paths 90 degrees. Align the two parallelograms so they form the two bottom sides of a cube.

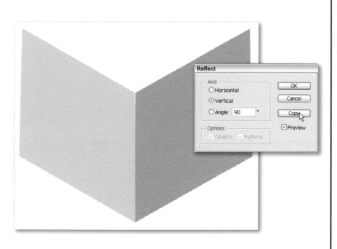

⑥ Apply a white fill to the left side of the cube, a gray fill to the right side, and a black fill to the top. Duplicate the cube to create eight columns and eight rows of cubes.

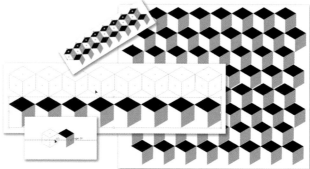

7 Draw a rectangle the same size as the grids you created in Task 14. Move that rectangle over the current set of cubes. You'll use it as a clipping mask.

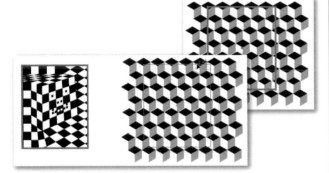

8 With the clipping mask rectangle and the underlying grid of cubes selected, press Command/Ctrl+7 to clip the grid.

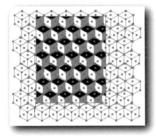

You create a face based on the same sized cube you created in the first section of this task. If you've made it this far, you're familiar with the technique: Create some 30-degree and –30-degree Guides, and space them about .3 inches. (Why such an odd increment? Just for fun.) You use the first cube as a *basis* for the face.

9 Draw a cube with a height (left side) of .3 inches. Make the sides black and white, and duplicate some of the sides.

10 You're now moving from rock and roll to jazz. I wish I could provide you with an effect to apply or an easy trick. Or, maybe I don't. In any case, freelance a distorted grid something like the one shown here.

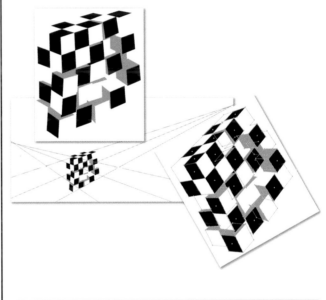

11 Change a smile to a frown . . . and warp it. Use small squares to re-do the digital happy face into a disjointed frown. Freelance.

12 Draw an outline around the box.

13 The final step in this task is to align the face you freelanced onto the grid of cubes. Select (and group) the cube face, and drag it onto the grid of cubes. Experiment with different locations. Aim for something that looks like the face is morphing out of the cubes.

14 After you tweak the location, touch up the face to help it morph smoothly into the grid of cubes.

NOTE

Because you grouped the face paths, they are a sublayer, and you can hide other layers to work on just the face. Toggle back and forth to see the face by itself, and the face on the grid. When finished, save the project as **morphs.ai**. You can combine this with the files you create in Tasks 14 and 16 for a montage.

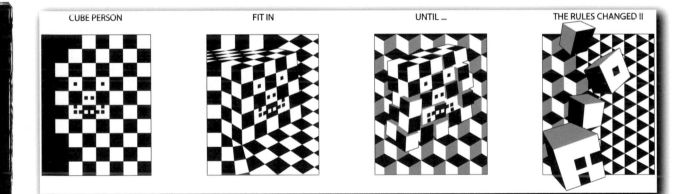

CUBE PERSON FIT IN UNTIL ... THE RULES CHANGED II

Escher Escapes

In this last "Escher" task, you learn to induce cognitive dissonance by disrupting your viewer's conception of squares and triangles. This project is the easiest of the trilogy. You create a background grid that is a combination of cubes and triangles — which works well as a morphing technique because triangles have three sides and cubes have six.

As with the previous two tasks, much of the work lies in setting up Guides. I'll dispense with the details of using 30-degree angle Guides to draw cubes (and triangles) because you've embedded that in your brain by now. But I will provide you with some useful advice on what kind of grid to set up.

WARNING

If you haven't created the morphs.ai file shown in Task 15, do that before moving onto this phase. If you have created that file, open it. You add the work in this task to the overall project.

1 Define a grid setting of ⁵⁄₃₂ inch. Create vertical Guides at: 0, ½ inch, ¾ inch, 1 inch, 1¼ inches, 1½ inches, 1¾ inches, 2 inches, 2⁵⁄₁₆ inches, and 2⁷⁄₁₆ inches.

2 Draw a rectangle 2½ inches wide, and 3 inches high, starting at the upper-left corner of the grid you created. This will be the border of the illustration.

3 Create a triangle (using the Polygon tool) with a radius of ⁵⁄₃₂ inch.

4 Rotate the triangle 60 degrees counterclockwise.

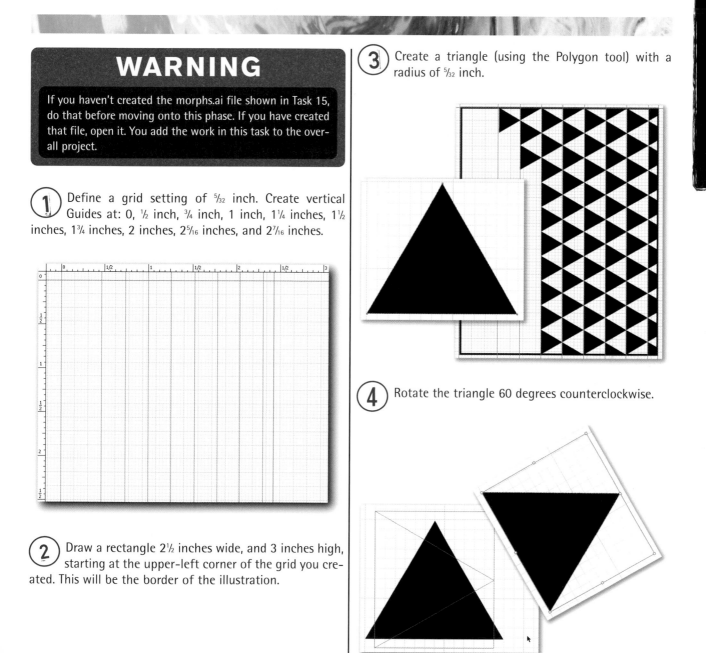

5 Fill the right six rows with copies of the triangle. Add three triangles to the top of the third column, and one triangle to the top of the second column, as shown.

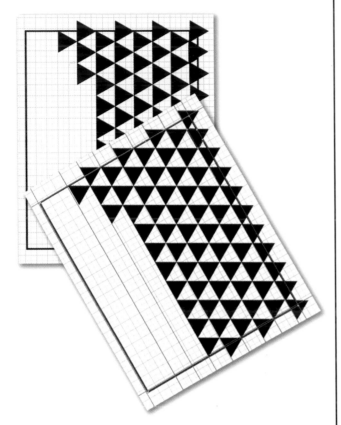

6 Truncate the triangles that extend beyond the border of the rectangle by selecting the triangle(s) and the edge of the rectangle that intersects the triangle, and using the Divide Pathfinder to split the triangle into two parts. Delete sections of triangles that protrude beyond the rectangle.

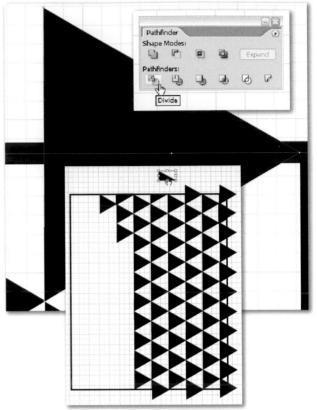

7 Create a cube starting with a ⁵/₁₆ inch line, and using 30-degree angles — a process you mastered in the previous task. Apply a gray fill to the right side of the cube, a white fill to the left side, and a black fill to the top. Using other techniques you are familiar with by now, fill the rest of the rectangle with black, white, and gray cubes. Divide cubes that extend beyond the rectangle and delete those portions.

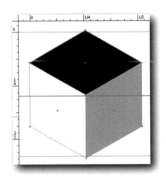

8 Draw three or four large cubes, and drag them onto, and protruding beyond the borders of the rectangle.

9 Polish up the illustration by adding a few small black rectangles to invoke the by-now demolished happy face at the beginning of the series of cubes.

Stolen Jewels

You can create a flashy jewel project out of nothing but basic shapes, combined with some creative and gradient transparency. In this project, you'll stack up stars and shapes, copying, rotating, and applying transparency to build the final ring.

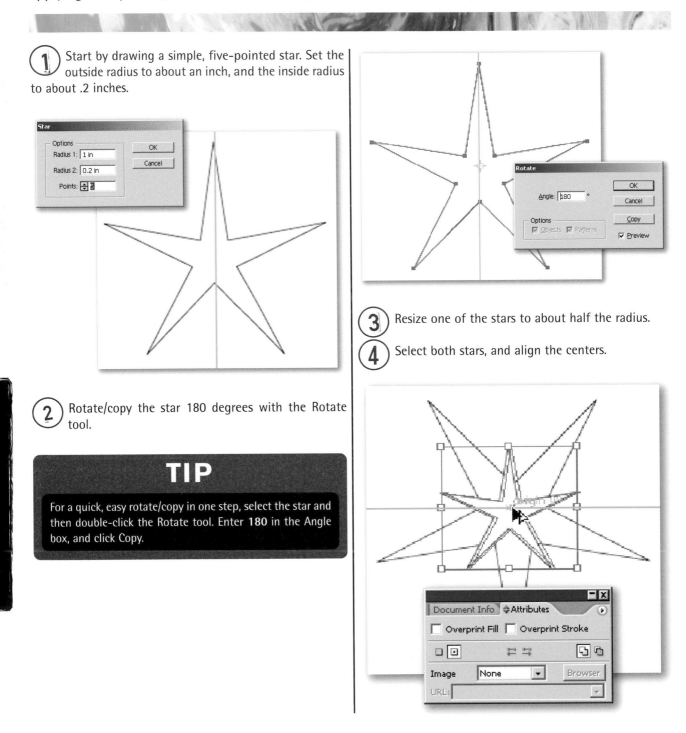

① Start by drawing a simple, five-pointed star. Set the outside radius to about an inch, and the inside radius to about .2 inches.

② Rotate/copy the star 180 degrees with the Rotate tool.

③ Resize one of the stars to about half the radius.

④ Select both stars, and align the centers.

TIP

For a quick, easy rotate/copy in one step, select the star and then double-click the Rotate tool. Enter **180** in the Angle box, and click Copy.

(5) Use the Merge Pathfinder tool to merge the two stars.

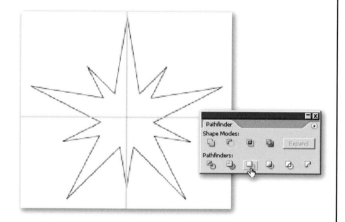

(6) Place a Radial Gradient–filled circle behind the merged stars. Define the inner gradient color at 90% cyan and 90% magenta. Set the Gradient Slider location for the inner color to 75%. Apply a black stroke to the circle. Then, center the circle under the stars (you can use the same centering shortcut I noted for Step 4).

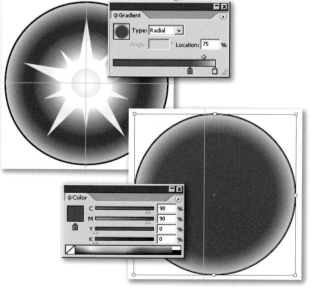

(7) Add a small circle in the middle of the gem. Apply any blue-to-white radial gradient to the small circle, and a yellow-to-white radial gradient to the star. Set the location of the white gradient stop to about 50%, and the location of the gradient midpoint diamond in the star to about 40%.

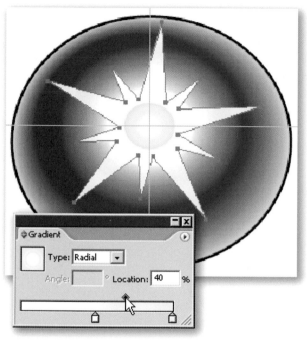

In this phase, you use the hexagon to generate much of the jewel bed. You start by drawing and rotating a hexagon, and then you rescale and copy to create the "steps" in the ring mounting.

(8) Use the Polygon tool to generate a hexagon with a radius of about 1.5 inches. Rotate the hexagon –5 degrees.

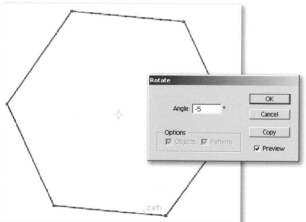

NOTE

Click the Scale Strokes and Effects checkbox in the Scale Tool dialog box so that the stroke thickness downsizes along with the hexagon.

9 Apply a non-uniform scale of 50% Vertical to the rotated hexagon.

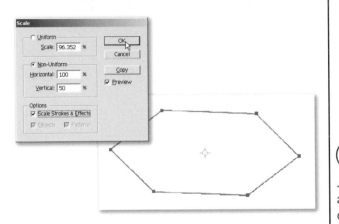

10 Apply a linear gradient fill to the hexagon, at a 63-degree angle. Set the gradient sliders *something like*:

* Left slider: 9% Cyan, 17% Magenta, 60% Yellow, no black.

* Right slider: 14.7% Cyan, 28% Magenta, 100% Yellow, and 20% Black.

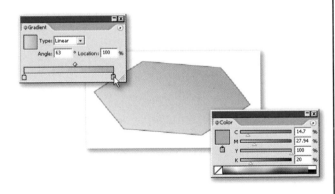

11 Finish the setting by copying and resizing a slightly smaller hexagon. Create an oval that fits inside the two hexagons. Apply a darker, solid gold fill to the second hexagon, and a darker brown fill to the oval. Center all three shapes, with the larger hexagon on the bottom, and the oval arranged on top.

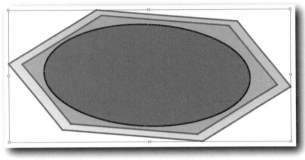

12 Begin to create the basic element of the band by drawing an ellipse about .125 inch wide, and about .4 inch high. Duplicate to create eight, vertically aligned and evenly spaced ovals (make the spacing about the width of the oval). Duplicate the row, and offset it slightly to the right (about the width of an oval). Align the bottom of the top row of ovals with the top of the bottom row.

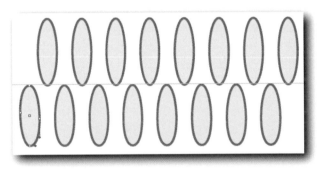

TIP

Feel free to freelance all you want on colors. The basic color scheme here is a gold band and a blue/turquoise jewel.

(13) Draw a rectangle over the ellipses, through the middle of the ellipses, cutting both the top and bottom rows in half (encompassing the bottom half of the top row and the top half of the bottom row). Make the rectangle wide enough to cover half of the ellipses on the ends of the bottom row.

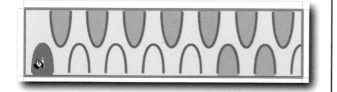

(14) With the rectangle and ellipses selected, choose Object ⇨ Live Paint ⇨ Make to transform the intersected lines into discrete paths. Use the Direct Selection tool to select and delete all the paths outside the rectangle. Use the Live Paint tool to paint all the semi-ellipses dark gold, and the rest of the rectangle light gold. Use something like 30% Cyan, 35% Magenta, 100% Yellow, and no Black for the dark gold (in the semi-ellipses), and something like 5% Cyan, 10% Magenta, 35% Yellow, and no Black for the light gold (in the rectangle).

TIP

If you haven't made the jump to CS2, and don't have Live Paint, use the Divide Pathfinder tool to slice off the parts of the ellipses that don't fit in the rectangle, and use the Direct Selection tool or Group Selection tool to delete them. It takes two taps on the Delete key to remove an object selected with the Direct Selection tool. It only takes one if you use the Group Selection tool.

(15) Assemble the base by duplicating and rotating the rectangle/ellipse shape, and aligning it with the three visible sides of the gem mounting. Apply a gradient fill to the ellipses.

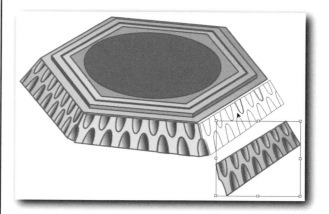

16 Add some sparkle to the mounting by placing some white stars on the mounting. Create these tiny stars the same way you created the glowing star in the first set of steps in this project.

17 All that remains for the ring is a band of gold, and some finishing touches for the gem itself. Feel free to tweak your gradients, add stars, and make sure everything fits right before finalizing the jewel.

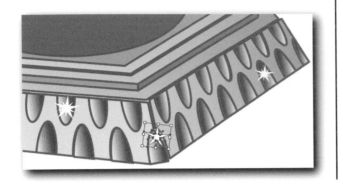

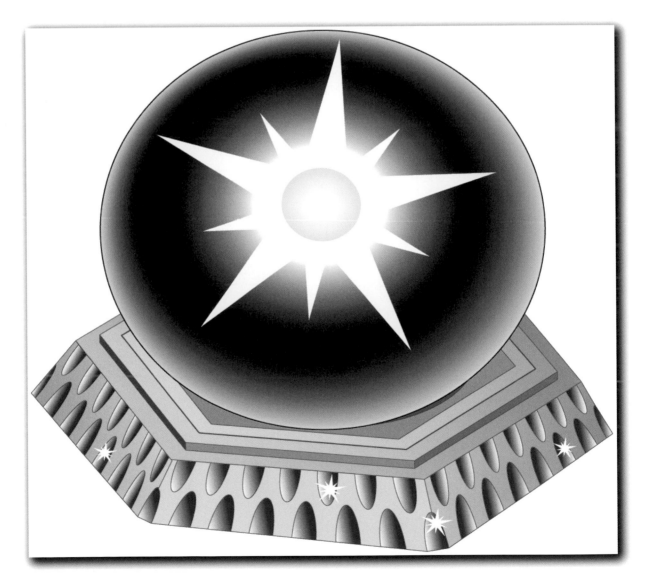

Band of Gold

Three-dimensional cylindrical bands are one of the more ubiquitous elements in Illustrator. In this project, I show you how to use Live Paint to easily create these symbols. As a graphical tribute to Freda Payne's song "Band of Gold," you create a digital gold band in this task. In the process, you'll draw a setting for the jewel you created in the previous task.

WARNING

If you haven't created the project in Task 17, do that before moving onto this phase.

(1) Create an ellipse, about 3.75 inch wide, and about 4.125 inch high. Fill it with 5% Cyan, 10% Magenta, 35% Yellow, and no Black.

(2) Rotate the ellipse about 45 degrees.

(3) Draw another ellipse about 2.9 inch wide, and 3.2 inch high. Duplicate the ellipse, and rotate both ellipses about 45 degrees. Align the two ellipses as shown.

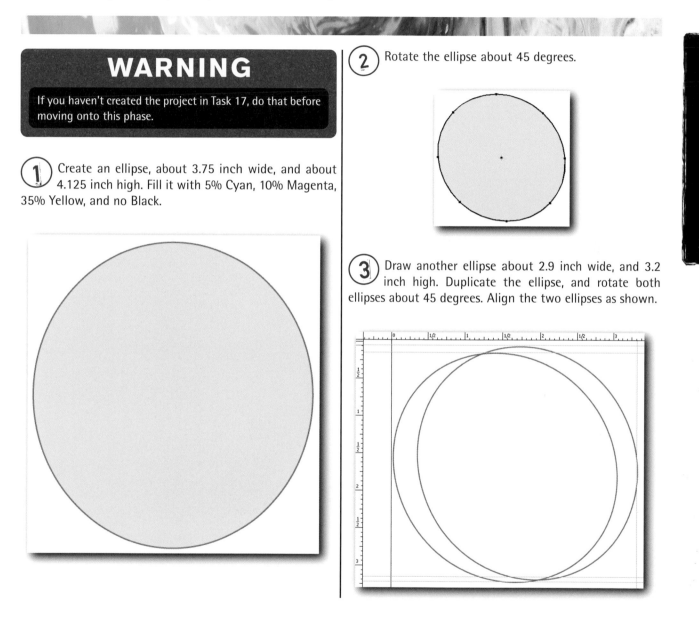

④ Align the three ellipses as shown.

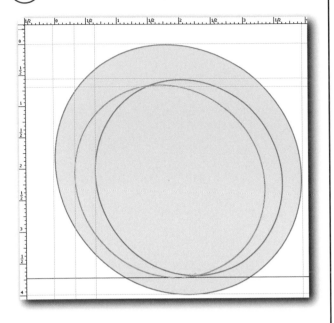

⑤ Select all three ellipses, and choose Object ➪ Live Paint ➪ Make to convert the intersecting regions into a Live Paint group.

⑥ Apply a white fill to the center of the Live Paint area.

⑦ Create a radial gradient fill with two gradient stops — one 9% Cyan, 17% Magenta, 60% Yellow, and no Black. The second stop with 15% Cyan, 30% Magenta, 100% Yellow, and 20% Black. Set the lighter gold stop at a location of 85%, and set the midpoint diamond to 60%. Apply this fill to the outer Live Paint region.

⑧ Create a linear gradient fill with the color stops at locations of 0% and 100%. Apply a mix of 5% Cyan, 8% Magenta, 30% Yellow, and 0% Black to the 0% color stop. Apply a mix of 15% Cyan, 30% Magenta, 100% Yellow, and 45% Black to the 100% color stop. Set the midpoint diamond to 60%, and the Angle to 105 degrees. Apply this gradient fill to the crescent-shaped Live Paint area on the left side of the ring.

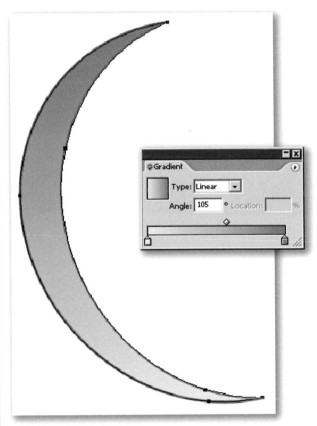

9 Add a bit of glitter with one of those stars you learned to create in Task 17.

10 Delete or apply no stroke color to strokes that should not be visible to finish the band.

Try combining the band with the jewel you created in the previous project.

bipolar photo effects

Yes, Photoshop can change a background, or add an effect. But it doesn't provide the range of Pen control, transparency effects, knockouts, Transparency Blend options, and clipping masks that you need to get *really* wild with photos.

There are essentially two ways you can integrate photo content into an Illustrator project. You can apply Live Trace to convert the photo to vectors, or you can use the photo as a placed template layer, and trace over it the old-fashioned way – with the Pen tool.

For most of the tasks in this chapter, it won't really be possible to extract useful vectors from Live Trace. Live Trace, as you saw in Task 11, for example, is amazing for projects such as traced line drawings and comic book art. In Task 20, for instance, you draw right over the photo with the Pen tool, and combine the Pen tool path with the underlying (or overlaid) photo.

Break Out

A fun Photoshop technique you find in every "Trix with Fotoshop" book shows someone stepping or jumping out of a picture frame. I love it. But Illustrator does that *so* much better.

For this, and the following project, you need to take a quick-and-dirty digital photo of yourself. So get your cell phone camera ready, and get a friend to pose for you.

1 Create a new file, and set Color Mode to RGB (choose File ⇨ Document Mode ⇨ RGB Color).

NOTE

You'll be using Photoshop effects that are available only in RGB color mode. If you find the steps that follow don't work, return to Step 1 and make sure your color mode is RGB.

2 Take a photo of yourself climbing out of something — like this.

3 Select File ⇨ Place, and navigate to the photo. Place the file in Illustrator as a layer, not as a template. Deselect the Link checkbox.

Removing Backgrounds – Photoshop vs. Illustrator Live Paint

Confession: The background in this photo was cleaned up with Photoshop. I haven't yet found or devised a technique with Live Paint that is even close to Photoshop for removing backgrounds.

Live Paint does an amazing job with scanned drawings and comics. And Live Paint is a major improvement in existing technology for vectorizing photos. Still, I find that it's much more effective to strip a photo background in Photoshop, and then apply Live Paint.

That makes sense. The one thing Photoshop is better at than Illustrator is finely tuned differentiation between pixels of different colors. Photoshop's Magic Wand tool can be tuned to differentiate a background color from other colors in a photo, making it easy to select and delete the background. Even more useful is Photoshop's Magnetic Lasso tool, that intuitively assists you in selecting the outline around an image, separating that image from the photo background.

If you are philosophically opposed to lowering yourself to using Photoshop, or you just can't spring the cash for a legal copy, take a photo of yourself against a clean white background, and resolve the problem of cleaning up the image background in that way.

4 Select the photo. Choose Effect ⇨ Artistic ⇨ Poster Edges, and apply settings like:

* Edge Thickness: 5
* Edge Intensity: 5
* Posterization: 3

Poster Edges	▼
Edge Thickness	5
Edge Intensity	5
Posterization	3

5 Duplicate the posterized photo.

TIP

In addition to creating a nice effect, posterizing makes it easy to create a clipping mask trace of the photo.

6 Use Live Trace to create a path around the entire figure on the top copy of the photo. Do that using the Control palette. With the photo selected, click the Live Trace button in the Control palette. Drag the Threshold slider all the way to the right to produce a single path around the figure. You'll be using this path as a clipping mask, so you don't want or need any photo detail.

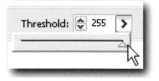

7 Click Expand in the Control palette to generate the vector trace. Make sure the vector version is on top of the photo. Ungroup everything that will make it easier to delete the bounding rectangle.

8 Create a crude, simple polygon with the Pen tool to create the shape through which you will "break out" of the photo.

9 With the crude polygon selected, choose Filter ⇨ Distort ⇨ Pucker & Bloat. Set the Pucker (formerly known as Punk) to about –50 to make a burst shape.

10 Apply no fill to the burst, and move the burst over the photo, and over the vector trace of the photo as well.

11 Apply an easy-to-see stroke color to the vector trace and no fill. You'll be using this as a clipping mask, so color isn't important.

12 Edit the path of the vector trace so that it conforms, on the bottom of the illustration, to the path of the burst.

13 Adjust the location of the traced path so that it is on the top of the photo, with the burst in back, and the photo in the middle.

14 Select everything except the burst. Select Object ⇨ Clipping Path ⇨ Make (or press Command/Ctrl+7).

15 Touch up:

* Apply a wacky gradient fill to the burst.
* Copy the mask shape, and paste it in back (behind everything). Apply a black stroke to the copy to clean up the edges of the figure.

Foto Fist Fights Back

Photorealistic vector images are used in some comics and illustrated novels, or as the basis for 3D modeling and animation. The technique of combining photo-realistic images with undisguised vectors is also found in all kinds of ads and illustrations.

In this project, you'll photograph and scan the fist, and then combine that with gradients, shapes, and other Illustrator goodies.

There is an existential aspect to this (of course) — which involves exploring the fine line between photos and drawings. Illustrations that cause the viewer to ask, "Is it a photo? Or a drawing?" attract attention and provoke interest.

Next Question: If you create a surreal photo-realistic fist, will it rebel? For insights into that existential dilemma, review the "Milagro – (6.18)" episode of *The X Files*, where an artist's creations come to life, with near-disastrous results.

This task should be less dangerous. It starts with a simple photo, adds a path, mixes in some gradient blend options, and gets spiced up with some relevant type.

WHAT YOU NEED

* You need a fist. Not a drawing of one, a real one — like yours.
* You need some kind of digital camera to take a picture of your fist, or someone else's.
* You need a message you want to share (or at least add to the project).

The first phase of this task involves combining a photo (later to be used as a transparency screen), with a Pen tool outline of the photo.

① Create a new file, and set Color Mode to RGB (choose File ➪ Document Mode ➪ RGB Color).

NOTE

You'll be using Photoshop effects that are available only in RGB color mode. If you find the steps that follow don't work, make sure you are working in RGB color mode.

② Take a photo of your own fist with a light shining on it to create a shadow against a white wall. Your cell phone will take a fine photo. Find someone with a hairier arm if necessary. Place the photo in a layer (not a template layer) without linking it.

TIP

Create a new file, choose File ➪ Place, and navigate to your file in the Place dialog box. JPEGs or TIFFs work fine. Don't place the file as a template layer because you are going to actually *edit* it — not just trace over it — in Illustrator. As noted in other discussions of embedding files, there's usually no upside to linking a photo that serves as a template for tracing.

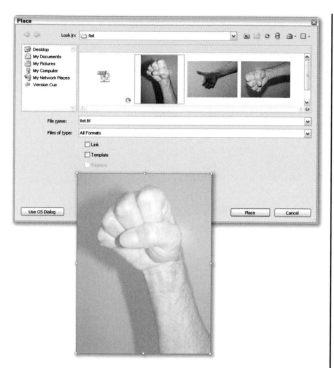

5 Select Effect ⇨ Sketch ⇨ Stamp. Set Light/Dark Balance to 25, and Smoothness to 1 for a grainy, high-contrast effect.

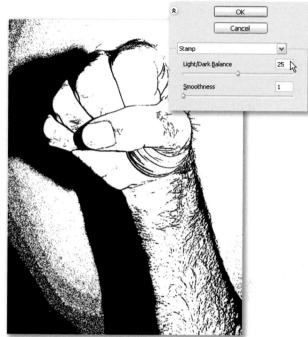

3 Select the photo on the artboard. A limited set of Photoshop effects becomes available from the Effects menu.

4 Choose Effect ⇨ Sharpen/Unsharp Mask. Define:

* ✱ Amount: 150%
* ✱ Radius: 0.1
* ✱ Threshold: 1.0

6 Use the Pen or Pencil tool to draw a closed path around the fist itself.

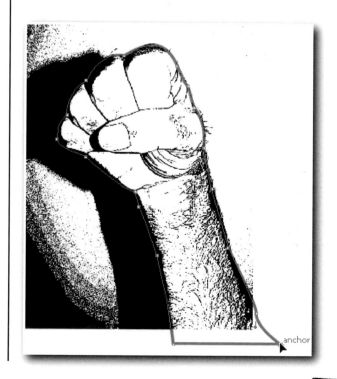

TIP

You can apply a stroke width and color to make tracing easier, but then apply no stroke to the path.

(7) Fill the path with any gradient. To access sets of preset gradient fills, choose Window ➪ Swatch Library and navigate to the Presets folder in the Adobe Illustrator CS2 program files folder. Double-click on Gradients to access a set of gradient fill swatch palettes.

(8) Send the gradient-filled path behind the photo. Then, create a background rectangle. Fill it with a different gradient.

Transparency vs. Transparency Blends

In this task, you're about to use Transparency Blend options. Most people think of transparency as simply limiting opacity (how much of an image shows through). But the Transparency palette can also be used to distort colors affected by the transparent object.

The action starts when you use the Overlay blend option in the Transparency palette to mesh the drawn fist with the photo. And the Difference blend option creates a chromatic digital dialectic.

Huh? Okay, here's how this works: The Overlay transparency blend option screens light colors, allowing a kind of clipping effect, while preserving dark elements. The Difference blend option in the Transparency palette transforms overlaid colors into their color-wheel opposites (blue becomes orange, black becomes white . . .).

9 Move the new rectangle behind everything.

10 Select the photo. In the Transparency palette (Shift+Command/Ctrl+F10), select Overlay from the pull-down menu. Leave the Opacity setting at 100, and do not select any of the checkboxes. Now that you can see the effect of the transparency overlay, adjust the colors of your gradients for a desired effect.

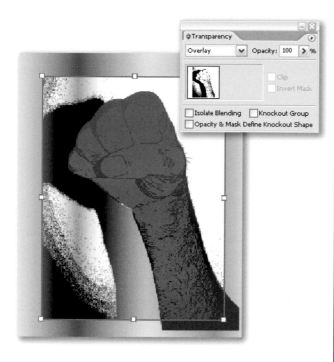

11 Type a message, and apply a solid color fill to the type.

12 With the type selected, view the Transparency palette (Shift+Command/Ctrl+F10). Select Difference from the Blending Mode popup menu. Leave the Opacity setting at 100, and do not select any of the checkboxes.

Touch up:

* Move and/or resize the background rectangle so it does not protrude from behind the photo on the top or left (only on the right and bottom).

* Now that you have applied effects, experiment with different gradient fills to see how they interact. Choose ones that produce the impact you want.

* Tweak the type color to coordinate with the rest of the color set.

This project is *really* one where you can't go wrong free-lancing gradient fills and colors. Therefore, I left those to your imagination in the steps for the task. However, if you must duplicate the exact color set in the preceding illustration, use these settings:

* Transparency for the fist: –90 degree Linear fill from solid red (on the left) to R-93, G-16, B-210. Angle Location: 100%.

* Transparency for the rectangle background: –90 degree Linear fill from solid yellow (R-255, G-255, B-0) to solid turquoise (R-0, G-255, B-255). Angle Location: 100%.

* Type: Solid yellow

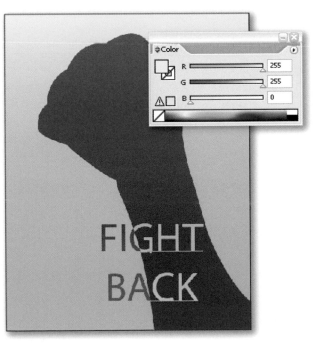

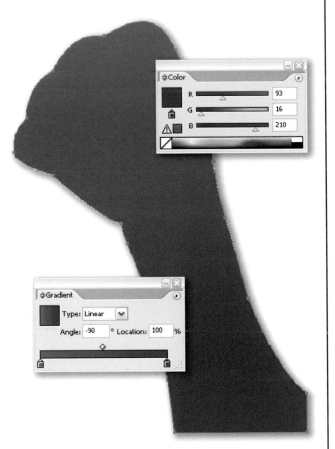

14 Edit the content of the message, and tweak colors and transparency.

All secrets are now revealed.

Sucked into a Black Hole

Still got your photo from Task 19? Good. If not, get out the cell phone/camera and do one more shot of you breaking out of something. Okay, you're ready now to get sucked into a black hole. In this task, you apply a Transparency Mask to clip a photo.

1 Create a new file, and set Color Mode to RGB (Choose File ⇨ Document Mode ⇨ RGB Color).

CAUTION

You use Photoshop effects that are available only in RGB color mode.

2 Select File ⇨ Place, and navigate to the photo. Place the file in Illustrator as a layer, not as a template. Deselect the Link checkbox.

3 Select the photo. Choose Filter ⇨ Blur ⇨ Radial Blur, and apply settings like:
  * Amount: 25
  * Blur Center: (as is, centered)
  * Blur method: Zoom
  * Quality: Good

4 Draw an ellipse that covers about the width and height of the photo.

5 Apply a radial black-to-white gradient fill with these settings:
  * Set the left gradient color stop to white.
  * Set the right gradient color stop to black.
  * Set the Type to radial.
  * Set the midpoint diamond at 50%.

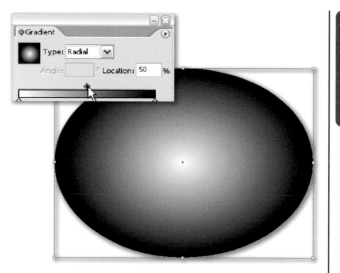

NOTE

The other checkboxes are only relevant if you are preparing this for commercial print output. If that were the case, you'd consult with your print people on which options worked best with their printing process.

(6) Duplicate the gradient-filled ellipse, and drag one copy over the photo. Center it.

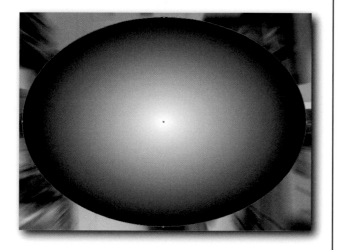

(9) Drag the second ellipse behind the photo.

(7) Select the ellipse and the photo. View the Transparency palette (Shift+Command/Ctrl+F10).

(8) From the Transparency palette fly-out menu, choose Make Opacity Mask. Use these settings in the Transparency palette for the opacity mask:

* Set Opacity to 100%.
* Select the Clip checkbox.
* Deselect the Invert Mask checkbox.

10 Tweak the illustration by playing around with the gradient fill and distorting the shape.

Or . . . combine it with the original photo!

Vector Portrait

Vectorized photos are a whole industry. Studios like VectorPhoto.com (www.vectorphoto.com) specialize in producing gleaming, slightly surrealized vector photos, or vector-like photos. Other vector portrait artists create less realistic, anime-like portraits. Vectorized portraits are also used for animation.

Vectorized portraits allow you to apply the whole range of Illustrator effects to a converted photo. Or not. Sometimes just the process of converting a pixel-based photo to a vector-based collection of paths creates an unusual and interesting image.

Illustrator Chris Nielsen fashioned just such a portrait from a photo of his son Jonah, and shared the process with me.

TIP

This project is a hybrid — you let Live Trace do some of the work, and draw many paths yourself. You can't *rely* on Live Tracing to create appropriate paths for the completed project. But a traced version of the photo won't hurt, and you will be able to use *some* of the generated paths. Mainly, however, you have to draw paths yourself. Therefore, you will create a template layer for manual tracing reference, *and* generate a Live Trace. The procedures and approaches in this task will work with any face photo.

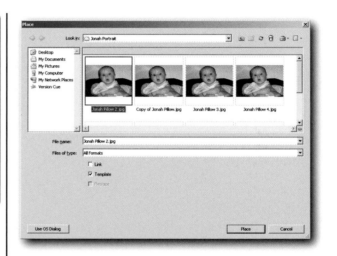

1. Create a new file in Illustrator.

2. Select File ⇨ Place, and navigate to a JPEG, TIFF, or other raster photo file (using either your operating system Place dialog box, or the Adobe dialog box).

3. Select the Template checkbox to import the photo as a non-editable template layer.

4. Deselect the Link checkbox — you won't want to interactively link the template layer image with changes you make to the source file. Click Place to place the photo as a template layer.

CAUTION

You cannot use Live Trace on a raster image placed in a template layer. By default, template layers are locked. You can, of course, unlock the template layer in the Layers palette, and then use Live Trace. However, this image doesn't lend itself well to Live Tracing because it is an uncompressed TIFF file with a lot of fine gradation in pixel color.

The purpose of tracing, again, is to get a bit of a head start, and use *some* of the generated paths as facial features. There is no need, or point, to worrying about color during this process. You supply color separately, making your own subjective decisions on recoloring, and tweaking that.

Because adding color is a separate step, when you trace, you will preview the outline, not the fill colors.

⑤ The placed raster portrait photo is in the template layer. It should stay there. Create a duplicate (editable) layer by selecting the layer in the Layers palette, and choosing Duplicate *your layer name* Layer from the Layers palette fly-out menu.

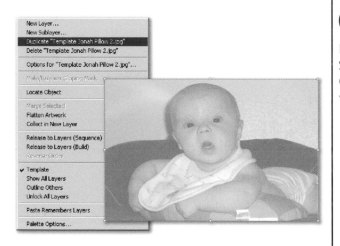

⑥ Double-click the new, copied layer in the Layers palette, and rename the new layer Traced Photo in the Layer Options dialog box.

⑦ Deselect the Template checkbox, and click OK in the Layer Options dialog box.

TIP

Deselecting the Template checkbox unlocks this layer, so it can be edited. You won't be able to apply Live Trace to the placed photo in a locked layer.

⑧ With the placed raster photo selected on the new (non-template) layer, click Live Trace.

NOTE

Unless you selected the checkbox to not show this warning, Illustrator cautions you that tracing a large, high-resolution image with lots of colors is going to "proceed slowly." My question is: Why decide *now* to warn us about a feature that will proceed slowly. Tracing high-resolution, multi-color photos takes a little time, but not as much time (or processing capacity) as applying many effects.

⑨ Toggle the Visibility *off* for the template layer to make it easier to preview Live Trace results. Set the Raster Preview option in the Control palette to No Image. Set the Preview Different Views of the Vector Result to Outlines. The focus is on getting useful paths; you don't want to be distracted by previewing fills.

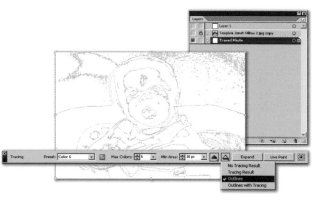

NOTE

The MAC Control palette for a selected photo has the same basic features as, but looks a little different than the pictured PC Control palette. There is only one arrow that lets you select presets or Tracing Option, which opens the Live Trace Options dialog box. Inside the View rectangle, you select "no image" from the Raster pull-down menu, and you can select Outlines from the Vector pull-down menu.

(10) From the Preset drop-down menu in the Live Trace Control palette, choose Color 6. The concept here is to minimize generated paths, while still getting a head start on your hand tracing work. Click Expand to generate paths from the photo. Organize layers so the traced layer is on top of the template layer, and examine the "head start" you achieved toward hand tracing.

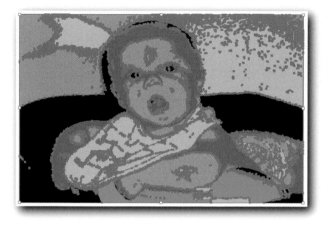

The heart of this project is good old-fashioned drawing and manipulating paths with the Pen tools. Use the Delete Anchor Point tool (select with –, the "minus" sign) liberally as you tweak generated paths into elements of the face. Use the Direct Selection tool (A) to move anchor points and to manipulate control points to change curve shape. And use the Convert Anchor Points tool (Shift+C) where necessary to convert straight line anchors to curves.

(11) To facilitate creating each element of the portrait, choose New Layer from the Layers palette fly-out menu, and create a layer for each significant element of the illustration.

(12) In the original traced photo layer, use Command/ Ctrl+Direct Selection tool to select all the elements of the mouth in the portrait. Copy to the clipboard.

(13) Select the Mouth layer, and paste the copied paths to the layer. Hide all layers except for the Mouth layer to verify the results.

(14) Repeat this process to copy useful paths to other layers. This is a bit tedious, but it's easier than drawing all elements of the face by hand.

(15) One by one, view each layer with an element of the face. Click the "bull's-eye" in the Layers palette to select all objects in the layer.

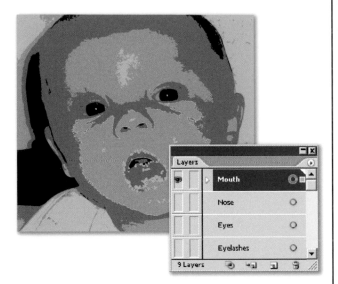

(16) Start cleaning up the trace-generated path by choosing Object ➪ Path ➪ Simplify. Click the Preview and Show Original checkboxes, and interactively experiment with Curve Precision (how closely to adhere to existing paths) and Angle Threshold (the minimum angle curve affected to delete unnecessary anchors). Click OK in the Simplify dialog box when you have a close approximation of the shape you want.

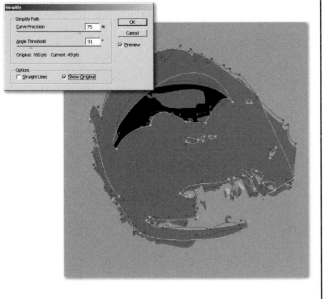

(17) Finally, use the Delete Anchors tool to remove unnecessary anchors that the Simplify dialog box didn't zap for you, and use the Direct Selection (A), Delete Anchors (-), and Convert Anchor Point (Shift+C) tools to move anchors and manipulate control points to finish each face part. Through this process, you'll reduce the number of anchors to something like 20 percent of those generated by the Live Trace, and you'll clean up and add a customizing touch to the photo.

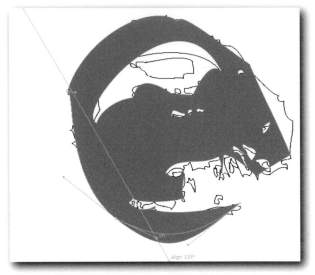

(18) The final step in turning the portrait into an Illustrator painting is to apply fill colors to each path. One useful technique (which works in Windows only in my version of CS2) is to open the original raster photo in another Illustrator window, and to tile the two windows (Window ➪ Tile). Use the Eyedropper tool to pick up colors from the original photo and apply them to the vector path fills.

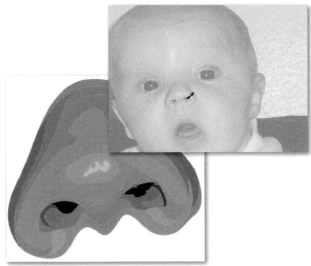

19 Of course a key element in creating the painted look is to customize coloring. Use the Color palette to tweak . . . or *more* than tweak . . . selected color fills.

Your result can be a wildly recolored portrait, or a more subtle, semi-photo realistic image.

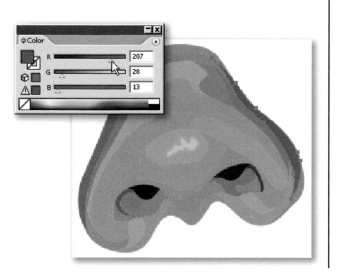

Jonah - 4 Months

fresh outta the blender

Step blends can be incredibly practical, time-saving tools. A picket fence, a set of steps . . . it's much easier to blend two objects than to create a bunch of intermediate ones. Okay, so much for talking about practical stuff; the point here is to get weird.

The two sets of step-blend tasks in this chapter involve a pretty cool trick for tweaking the spacing of step blends between different sized objects. It involves fiddling with the length and direction of the Control Point Handles in the blend spine. To rather interesting effect, I think you'll agree.

Stick Man Evolves and Devolves

Devo made a career in the eighties cashing in on the whole de-evolution thing. (Remember "Whip It"?) This Evo-Devo project is a recognition that things don't go in a straight line. And, ironically, it's all done with straight lines.

If you can draw a stick figure — in Illustrator at least — you can do this project. You draw a stick figure, and group him (her?, it?). You generate simple step blends using the figures, and reflected versions of the figures.

The second phase of the project involves aligning the blends on spiral splines. But first, you symbolize evolution and de-evolution with blends.

The final result of this project is created by stringing together a number of step blends. To the average viewer, they'll look like one long blend (if the "average viewer" even knows what a blend is). But, in fact, this extended blend is created by sticking together a bunch of step-blend segments.

Each blend is a four-step blend. I walk you through that a bit, but the blend part is easy because every blend in this project is the same. After you create each figure, and before you blend, you group each figure.

These stick figures are drawn mostly with the Line tool, and a little bit with the Pencil or Pen tool (you pick, either one will do). You might use the Ellipse tool (plus a little rotation) to make the heads. For figures that get spun around, you use the Reflect tool.

Like most of the tasks in this book, precision is irrelevant. You're not drawing the plans for a nuclear power plant; these are stick figures.

(1) Start out by defining step-blend options in four steps.

TIP

Double-click the Blend tool in the Tools palette. In the Blend Options dialog box, select Specified Steps from the Spacing menu, and enter 4 in the Steps box, and select the Align to Path alignment option.

(2) Draw the first stick-man figure. Group all the paths (select the whole figure, and click Command/Ctrl+G).

(3) To create the second figure, copy the first figure, and modify it using the Direct Selection and Rotation tools. Group all the paths.

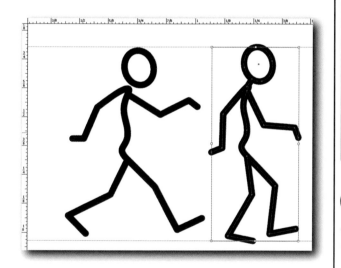

(4) Before you blend, *duplicate* the first stick figure *twice.* You'll use him again, and again.

(5) Space the two figures horizontally so that there is space for four blended figures in between them. Keep them on the same basic horizontal plane.

(6) Generate a four-step, step blend by selecting the Blend tool (press W), and clicking first in the middle of the figure on the left, and then in the middle of the figure on the right.

(7) Prepare the second blend group. Start with your duplicate of the second stick figure in the first group, and draw this additional figure. Group the new figure (don't group both figures into a group).

⑧ Make a copy of the new figure; you use him shortly.

⑨ Create a four-step, step blend between the original figure and the new one.

⑩ Blend the last (third) stick figure back into the first one.

⑪ Draw these two figures, spaced as shown.

⑫ Duplicate the first figure you drew. You use him/her/it in the second phase of this project.

⑬ With the Blend tool (W), click first in the middle of the first new figure, and then in the middle of second new figure.

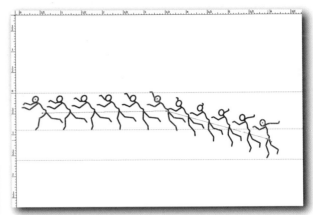

⑭ Draw a final stick person figure, and create another four-step blend.

The second set of blends will devolve humans back into . . . antelopes? Okay, this is art, not science. Therefore, we can reverse evolution and goof around with what evolved into whom.

It will be easier to create these figures with the Pen or Pencil tools because they involve more smooth anchors and curved paths than the stick people. But, like the stick people, feel free to be imprecise.

⑮ If you're re-starting here, make sure step blend options are set at four steps, and that the blend orientation is set to Align to Path.

⑯ Select the copy of the first dancing figure you drew in Step 11, in the previous section of this task (the guy you duplicate in Step 12). Double-click the Reflect tool, and copy/reflect the figure vertically.

TIP

If you forget to duplicate the first figure you drew, you can extract any of your blended figures by copying the whole blend, and then choosing Object ⇨ Blend ⇨ Release (Option/Alt+Shift+Command/Ctrl+B) to break up the blend. Select and delete the blend spline (the line that defines the path of the blend) that is a leftover from the blend. You can now work with either of the blended objects individually.

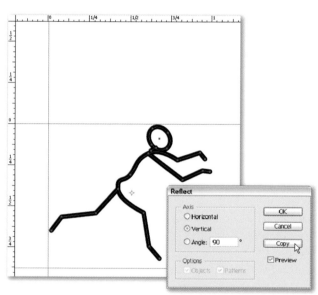

17 Using the illustration and spacing shown, create a second figure to which you will devolve the dancing human. Copy the second figure; you use it shortly to continue the cycle.

18 Generate a four-step, step blend by selecting the Blend tool (press W), and clicking first in the middle of the figure on the left, and then in the middle of the figure on the right.

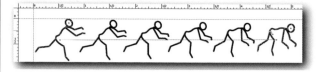

19 Use the devolved human you created in Step 3. Add the further devolved animal shown here, and space as shown.

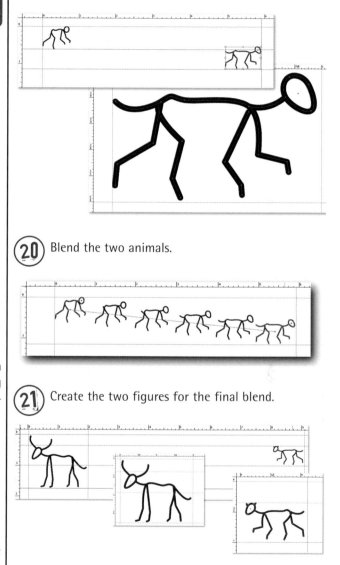

20 Blend the two animals.

21 Create the two figures for the final blend.

22 Blend the two figures.

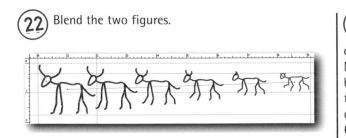

23 Your ten evolutionary and de-evolutionary blends will get spiraled in the next task. For now, you've created a pre-historic cave painting with the ten blends. Move the grouped blended pairs around the artboard, but keep them in the basic order in which you created them. Assign different colors to strokes, and some fills to create blended colors as well as shapes. You can use the Group Selection tool to select just one of two blended paths.

Evo-Devo Revolves

A blend generated on one path can be *realigned* on *another path*. This under-appreciated technique can be used to adhere blends on *any* path — including a curve or a spiral. Transferring a blend from one path to another, however, often throws the even spacing between generated objects out of whack. So, there's always a bit of tweaking involved after you transplant a blend from one path to another.

You get to see how all that works in this task, when you transfer the strings of blended stick figures you created in Task 23 onto a spiral and rescale them.

The three phases of this project are

* Create the spiral path.

* One by one realign the blends to segments on the spiral path.

* Resize the blended figures to scale them proportionally to the expanding spiral.

1 Draw and center four circles with diameters of 8, 6, 4, and 2 inches.

2 Draw a horizontal line with no stroke thorough the center of concentric circles. Select the line and the circles, and click the Divide tool in the Pathfinder palette to split the circles into semicircles. Alternately, you can select the (soon to be) flat side anchor of each semicircle with the Direct Selection tool and press Delete.

CAUTION

The illustration you create in Step 2 shows a line with a stroke — that's just to make it easier for you to see. Apply no stroke to the line.

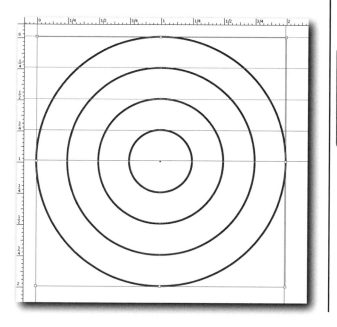

3 Use the Group Selection tool to select two concentric circles at a time. Offset them to create spirals.

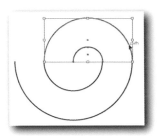

4 Continue building the spiral arcs to complete a four-arc spiral.

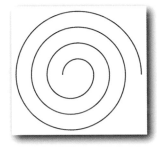

5 Rotate the spiral 90 degrees.

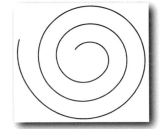

6 Use the Scissors tool to break the spiral into independent parts. You end up with 12 distinct paths that will serve as spines for the blended shapes. You are starting with discreet semicircles, so you need to cut them at their midpoints. The last outside paths are bigger than a quarter circle, so for them, you can join an existing quarter circle path and cut as needed.

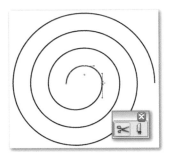

Replacing Spines

The next phase in this project is to replace the *spines* — the lines that define the path of a blend — with the arcs on the spiral. Every blend has a spine. This is an invisible path that defines how the blend travels from the first to the second blended object.

Illustrator allows you to replace the original spine — in your case the default straight lines that got generated for your four-step blends — with any other path.

As you transfer the blends from their straight paths onto any kind of arc or spiral, you need to rotate the blended objects to make them align properly to the path onto which they are adhered.

In this task, each blend starts with a repeat of the figure that ended the previous blend. This means that you're going to place the first figure of the next blend on top of the last figure of the previous blend — over and over until all ten blends are placed on the spiral. I'll show you the rotation technique involved, but first, apply the first blend set to the spiral.

7 Select the first blended group you created, and select the innermost path segment in the spiral.

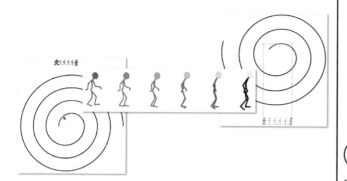

8 With both the *blended group* (which is not yet on the spiral) and the spiral segment selected, choose Object ➪ Blend ➪ Replace Spine.

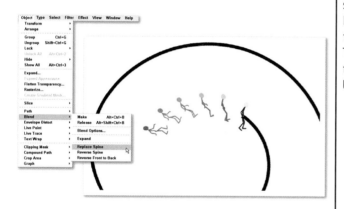

9 The first one was easiest because it doesn't have to align with a previous group. The remaining sets require some rotation. Adjust the rotation on the blend figures in the first blend to align the blend properly on the arc. Select the second blended group, select the second arc in the spiral, and replace their spine with the spiral segments using the same Object ➪ Blend ➪ Replace Spine technique.

10 The first figure in the second blend group is not aligned with the last figure in the first blend group — either in color, or in alignment. So, the next trick is to match the color of the last figure in the first blend with the coloring in the first figure in the second blend. To do that, double-click the first figure in the second blend set with the Group Selection tool to select the entire stick person. With the stick figure selected, press I to access the Eyedropper tool, and with that tool, Shift-click on the *last* figure in the *first set* of figures to pick up the stroke color. The stroke coloring is now matched. It's okay (fine, even) if the head fill color differs; that fits into a smooth segue between the two groups.

11 Match location and rotation angle. With the first figure in the second group still selected, use the Direct Selection tool to drag an easy-to-find point, like the back heel anchor, on the selected figure so it matches that on the figure it is supposed to fit on top of.

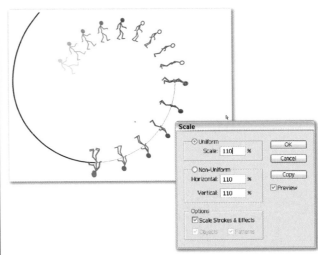

13 Using the same steps as in the previous section of this task, attach the third set of blended figures to the next arc segment in the spiral.

12 With the figure still selected (double-click with the Group Selection tool if necessary to reselect the whole figure), press R for the Rotation tool. By default, the rotation pivot point is in the center of the stick figure. Change that by clicking on the heel anchor (or whatever anchor you used to align one anchor in the two figures). Use the Rotation tool to drag on the head of the stick figure so that the two stick men are aligned exactly the same.

14 Select the last figure in the third set. Double-click on the Scale tool to open the Scale dialog box. Make sure the Scale Stroke & Effects checkbox is checked in the Scale dialog box. Apply a Uniform Scale to increase the selected figure by 110 percent

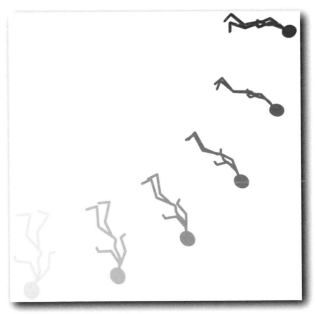

You use this same routine to connect the third grouped set to the second, the fourth to the third, and so on. But for the third group on, you will also adjust the scaling of the new blends.

The first two blended sets have been placed in the inner most segments of the spiral. Those are the shortest arcs. As you head toward the outside of the spiral, the arcs get longer and there is more height as well for the figures.

So, after the first two sets of figure blends, and starting with the end of the third set, each set ends up 10 percent bigger than it started. You'll do this by scaling the *final* figure in the blend to 110%, and then making the next set 10 percent larger than the previous one.

15 Using Steps 7 and 8 of this task, attach the fourth set of blended figures to the next arc segment in the spiral.

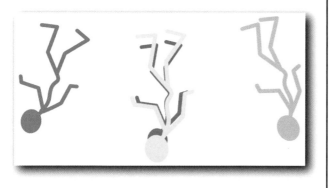

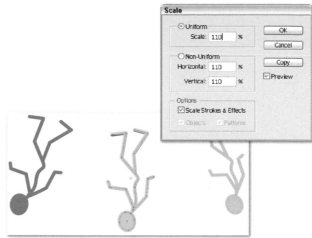

NOTE

The first figure in the new set will be 10 percent too small to match the figure it is supposed to fit with. The next step is to enlarge the first figure in the new set to match the last figure in the previous set.

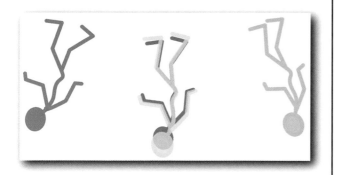

16 Select the first figure in the new blend set (by clicking twice with the Group Selection tool). Double-click the Scale tool, and uniform scale the new figure to 110%.

At this point, you've got the whole routine down. Each new set gets aligned with the previous set in size, and optionally color. Add all ten sets of blended figures to the spiral.

Complete the illustration by adding a black background and type. The type adds a label, and also compensates for the fact that there are twelve segments in the spiral, and only ten sets of blended figures.

17 Select the Type on a Path tool.

18 Click on the spiral path with the Type on a Path tool – after the end of the last set of blends – and type a label for the illustration.

19 Double-click the type to select it all, and apply an appropriate font, such as 72 point Stencil Bold.

20 Apply a bright color or white to the type.

21 Center a black circle behind the spiral, and your image is complete.

Winding Steps

In general, I've avoided like the plague connecting the techniques you're experimenting with, with anything practical or useful. But here, I can't resist pointing out that the method of adjusting the spacing along a spine of blends between differently sized, duplicated objects has a lot of practical uses, including when you are combining blends with perspective. That said, follow these steps to create the step-blended steps.

Everyone knows you can easily generate a step blend between two objects. By keeping the first and last objects simple (like the stick figures you played with in Tasks 23 and 24), the blends won't go too crazy on you.

In the previous tasks, you aligned blends on a curved spine by replacing the default straight-line spine with an arc. A less-known but pretty crazy trick is to tweak the *Control Point Handles* for the beginning and end of a blend spine. You'll do that here to create a winding staircase.

The first part of this project is to create a step blend of stairs. The beginning is easy — draw a step, duplicate it, and blend the two. The interesting part comes when you decrease the size of the second step to create perspective and then adjust the spacing of the step blend to correctly space the differently sized steps.

(1) Create a stair using the dimensions shown. Group the three pieces.

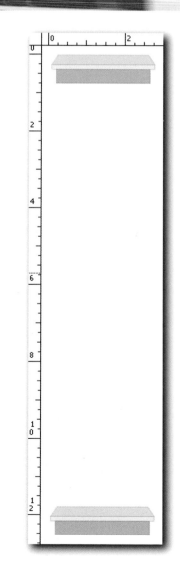

(2) Duplicate the stair, and place the copy about 12 inches above the original — for now.

3 Set blend options to 24 steps (Object ➪ Blend ➪ Blend Options). Define orientation as Align to Page. Select both stairs and press Option/Alt+Command/Ctrl+B to blend the two steps.

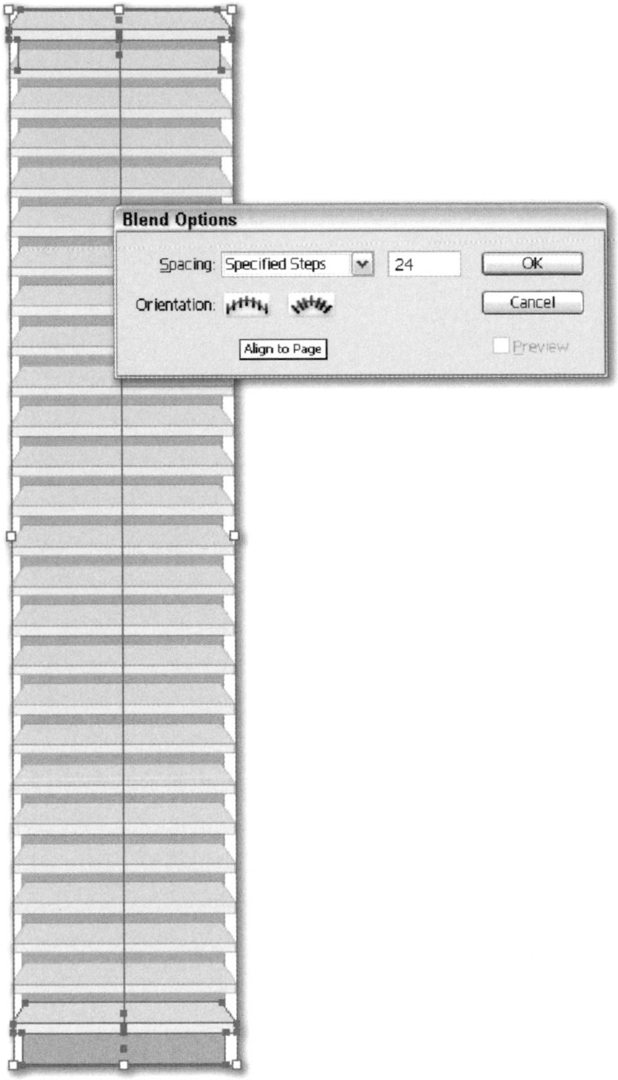

Blend Options

Spacing: Specified Steps ▾ 24   OK

Orientation: ⬚ ⬚   Cancel

Align to Page   ☐ Preview

4 Click twice on the top step with the Group Selection tool to select the step. Double-click on the Scale tool in the Toolbox, and scale the top step to 50% (uniform). Use the Preview checkbox, and experiment with larger scaling — choose an increment that looks good.

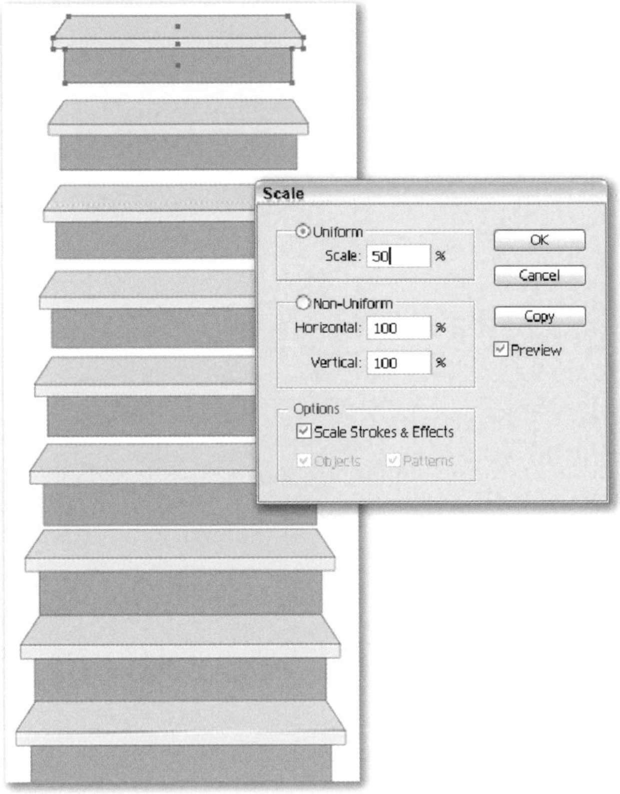

Scale

⦿ Uniform
Scale: 50 %   OK

○ Non-Uniform   Cancel
Horizontal: 100 %   Copy
Vertical: 100 %   ☑ Preview

Options
☑ Scale Strokes & Effects
☑ Objects   ☑ Patterns

(5) Scale the bottom step to 150% uniform.

Scale

○ Uniform
　Scale: [150] %

○ Non-Uniform
　Horizontal: [150] %
　Vertical: [150] %

Options
☑ Scale Strokes & Effects
☑ Objects　☑ Patterns

[OK]
[Cancel]
[Copy]
☑ Preview

(6) With the bottom step still selected (or use the Group Selection tool to reselect it if necessary), drag down (hold down the Shift key) to extend the blend until the entire last two steps are completely visible and do not overlap.

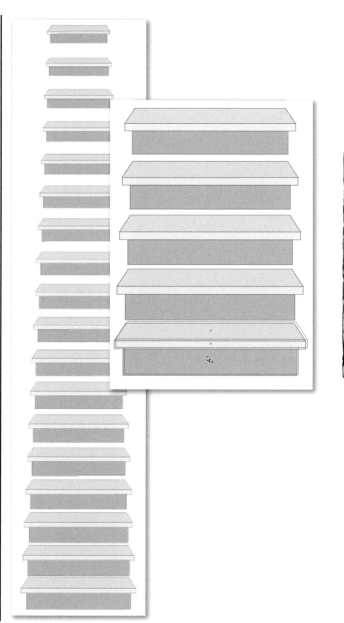

⑦ With the Direct Selection tool, select the (invisible) blend spine.

TIP

It might be easier to jump into Outline view (toggle back and forth with Command/Ctrl+Y) to select the blend spine. Toggle back into Preview mode to continue, as you can't see what's going on with the blend in Outline view.

⑧ Use the Convert Anchor Point tool (Shift+C) to select the anchor point at the bottom of the spine. Drag up on the anchor point to create a control point handle. Drag straight up on the top control point handle in the anchor until the spacing for the steps is somewhat *close to* even for the steps.

Next, you add an anchor point to the middle of the blend spine, and manipulate the new anchor control points to create what would be a chiropractor's nightmare if it were an unadjusted back.

As noted, in the first pair of tasks in this project, you created the arcs first, and then replaced the original blend spines with those arcs. Here, you're achieving somewhat similar results, but with a whole different approach. You're going to manipulate the curves in the existing spine. The result is an interesting twist in the staircase.

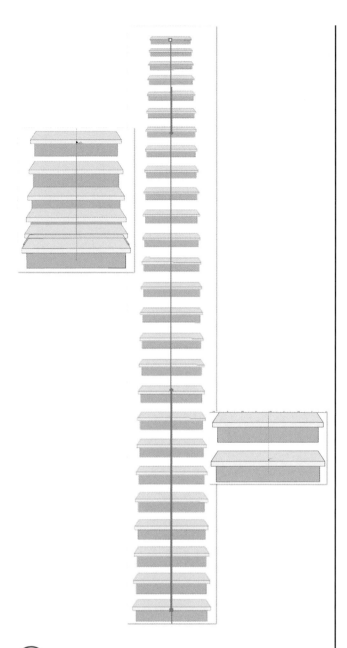

9) Select the curve spine from the step blend you just created. Outline view might make that easier because the spine is invisible.

TIP

After you get comfortable working with blend spine paths, you can pretty much guess where the path runs, and with the help of Smart Guides (toggle on and off with Command/Ctrl+U) you can select the spine with the Direction Selection tool in Preview mode. If you do jump into Outline view (toggle in and out with Command/Ctrl+Y), return to Preview mode for the next step.

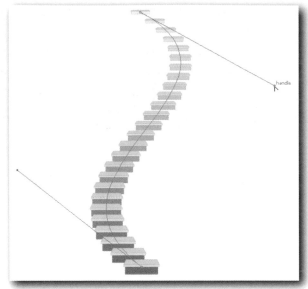

10 Use the Convert Anchor Point tool to rotate the control point handle on the bottom spine anchor to the left, as shown, to change the spine to a curve.

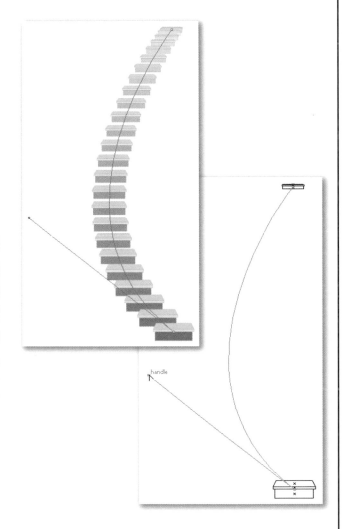

12 Tweak the control point handle lengths so that the distance between the steps along the path is *more or less* even.

13 Using a combination of tweaking the length of the control point handles on the spine, and moving the top step in small increments, align the stairs so they more or less fit together.

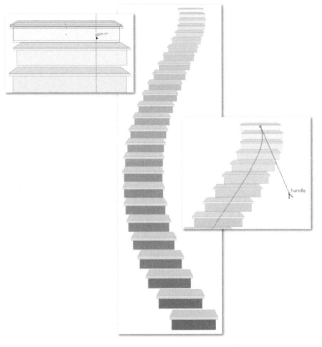

11 Use the Convert Anchor Point tool to manipulate the control point handle on the *top* spine anchor to convert the spine to an s-curve, as shown.

TIP

As you are being loose with the stair alignment, and some stairs overlap, you might need to select Object ⇨ Blend ⇨ Reverse Front To Back to move one step in front of another. This depends on whether you created the top, or bottom stair first.

(14) Add perspective by moving the top-right anchor point on the top step to the left, and the top-right anchor point in the bottom step to the right (use the Direct Selection tool).

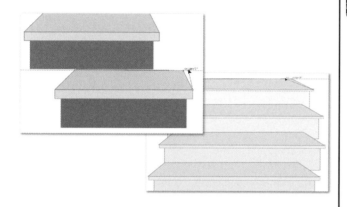

(15) When you finish tweaking the curve and the spacing of the steps, apply a gradient fill to the front of the steps to simulate shadows. Save the staircase for the next task.

Playing with Blend Spines

Even more than some of the tasks in this book, there's no "right way" to configure your curved steps. In a real-world situation, you would pay close attention to having the steps align perfectly, but here you're trying to skew around with the step path.

You can play with:

- The curve of the blend spine (by rotating the control point handles)
- The spacing of the steps (by adjusting the *length* of the control point handles)
- The blend itself (by tweaking anchor points on the beginning and end step

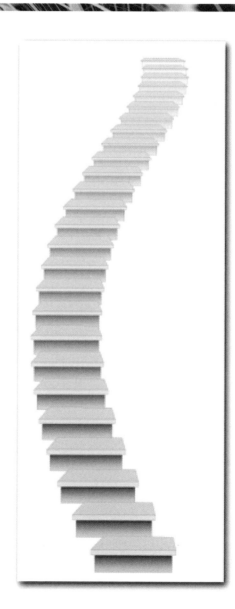

Stairway to Somewhere

In this task, you combine both gradient fills and smooth blends to create a tunnel-like shape. It's a fine line between gradient fills and smooth blends. Both techniques can be used for perspective, to portray rounded surfaces, and for other effects. Just like it's a fine line between being "inspired" by a song, and ripping off the tune.

In that spirit, I borrow a song title from Page and Plant for this task. (The guitar intro to "Stairway to Heaven" was itself apparently inspired by "Taurus," a song by the band Spirit).

Okay. The metaphor (gradient fills and smooth blends . . . being inspired by a song and ripping it off) is a little tortured, but the point here is that sometimes a smooth blend works best to generate depth, and sometimes a gradient fill works best. In this task, you use both to create a cave-like effect.

Phase 1 of this project is to create a step blend between two gradient-filled circles. Then, you use the technique you've explored earlier in this chapter — fiddling with control point anchor lengths to adjust the spacing of step blends.

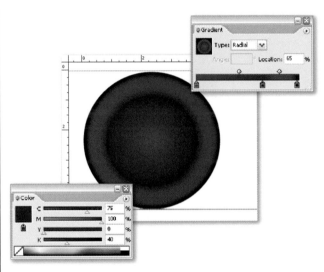

1. Draw a circle with a radius of 2.25" or so.

2. Fill the circle with a radial gradient. Use these settings to duplicate the gradient shown:

   * Left Gradient Stop: Location=0%, C=75%, M=100%, Y=0%, K=0%

   * Middle Gradient Stop: Location=65%, C=75%, M=100%, Y=0%, K=40%

   * Right Gradient Stop: Location=100%, C=0%, M=0%, Y=0%, K=100%

   * First (from left) midpoint diamond location=65%

   * Second (from left) midpoint diamond location=50%

3. Draw a small circle with a radius of about .45 inches, and center it at the bottom of the first circle.

NOTE

For the colors in this task, I'm using CMYK. To duplicate the colors shown, set your document color mode to CMYK (the color mode used for preparing printed output). Do this by choosing CMYK from the Color palette menu.

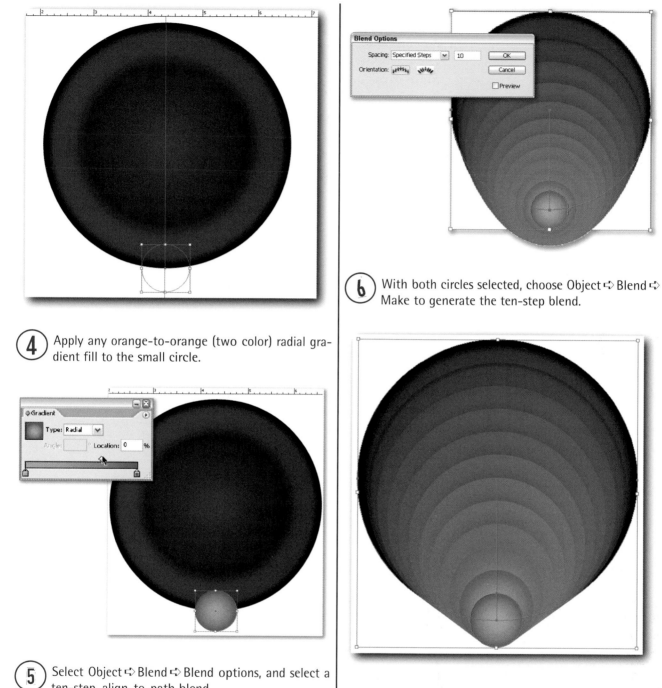

6 With both circles selected, choose Object ⇨ Blend ⇨ Make to generate the ten-step blend.

4 Apply any orange-to-orange (two color) radial gradient fill to the small circle.

5 Select Object ⇨ Blend ⇨ Blend options, and select a ten-step, align-to-path blend.

7 Use the Convert Anchor Point tool (Shift+C) to generate control point handles on both ends of step blend spine.

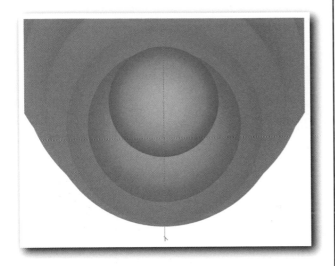

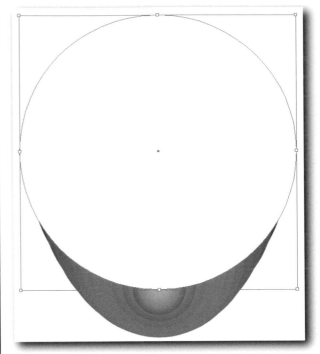

8 Drag up and down on the control points to adjust the length of the handles, and adjust spacing between circles so that the bands formed by the step blend grow slightly wider as they extend away from the small circle.

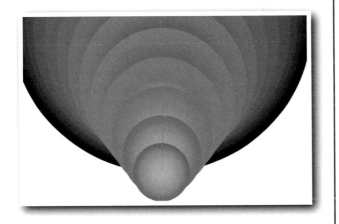

9 Next, you create a circular clipping mask to crop out everything that extends beyond the original small circle. Draw a circle the same size as your original large circle (with a radius of 2.25 inches or so) and center it over the original large circle.

10 Select the new circle, plus the blend, and press Command/Ctrl+7 to apply the top circle as a clipping mask.

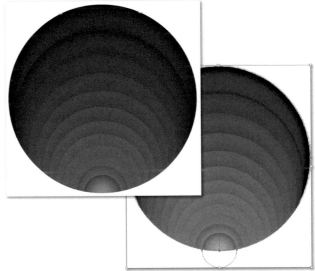

Now it's time to get a little crazy. You distort the masked objects by applying a transparency overlay.

11 Draw another copy of (or copy) the large circle.

12 Paste the copy in front of the masked blend.

13 Fill the new circle with purple.

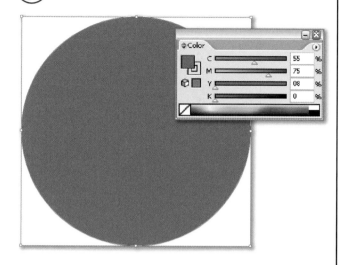

14 With the new circle selected, select Overlay from the pull-down menu in the Transparency palette. Leave the Opacity slider set to 100%.

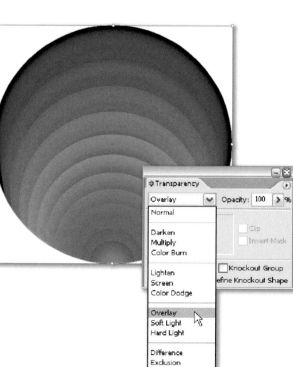

15 You can touch up your tunnel to hell by experimenting with the color of the top circle. Try red. Or, a gradient. Place a black background behind the tunnel, and stare at it for a really, really long time. Or, experiment with different modes from the Blending Mode pull-down menu in the Transparency palette.

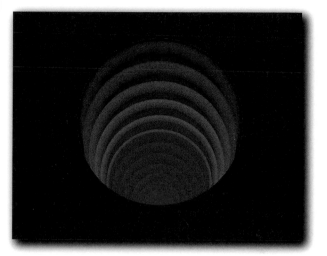

16 Connect the winding stairs from the previous task to your tunnel to hell.

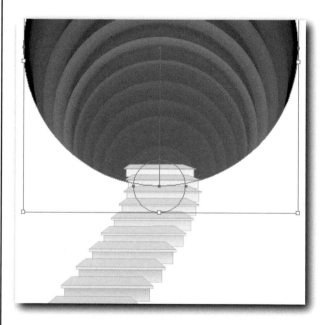

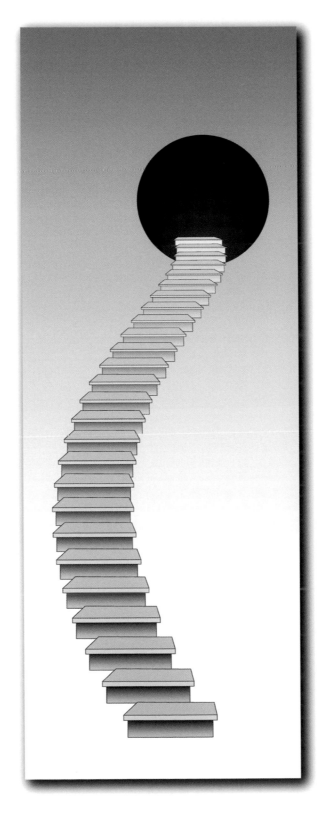

blends on speed

Now the boys all thought I'd lost my sense
And telephone poles looked like a picket fence
They said, "Slow down! I see spots!
The lines on the road just look like dots
   – Commander Cody and His Lost Planet Airmen, "Hot Rod Lincoln"

In Chapter 5, you experimented with curved, distorted, and wigged-out step blends. In this chapter, I show you ways to stretch the speed limit on smooth blends. There is an existential angle to note here: There's no such thing as a completely smooth blend. What Illustrator calls smooth blends are just blends with lots and lots of steps so that they look smooth. Because I'm focusing on effect, not technical junk, here some of the "smooth" blends you'll be working with are actually step blends. But the effect is a whoosh, not a step.

The other theme here is speed. In our book *PC Magazine Guide to Printing Great Digital Photos* (Wiley, 2005), Bruce Hopkins and I began to play around with ways of conveying speed. Photoshop has its filters, but Illustrator vectors open up unique and more extreme options for creating the illusion of motion. You accelerate through a series of speed experiences in the tasks in this chapter, all of which lead to a Volkswagen Minibus speeding down the freeway.

Motion Sickness on the Freeway

The first phase in this series of tasks is to create a freeway surface blended to put the viewer in a state of panic, vertigo, motion sickness, disorientation, and nihilistic acceleration. You accomplish that by combining sets of blends to merge a freeway with a background sky.

Color specs for many of the tasks in this chapter are RGB, so it might be convenient to choose File ⇨ Document Mode ⇨ RGB now.

(1) Create two horizontal and two vertical Guides to define an area *about* 12¼ inches wide and *about* 8 inches high.

NOTE

None of the dimensions in this project are anything like critical, so I won't emphasize that over and over again. If you're the kind of person who follows the recipe in a cookbook closely (or carefully learns sheet music parts for your band . . .), follow along with me closely and use my dimensions. Deviate all you like, but some of this gets a little crazy so you might do better sticking with my dimensions to make everything fit.

TIP

To create the three horizontal Guides from the ruler first, unlock the Guides (Option/Alt+Command/Ctrl+;). View the Info palette (F8). Select one of the Guides. Press R to select the Rotation tool, and click once where the Guide intersects the left vertical Guide you created in Step 1 to define the rotation pivot point. Then, with the Rotation tool still selected, drag up anywhere on the selected Guide until the Info palette shows the desired rotation angle. You use these Guides soon as a framework for defining perspective.

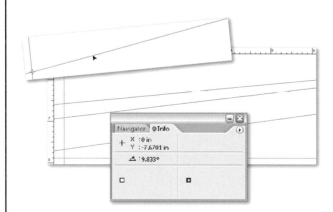

(3) Draw a rectangle starting at the top of the Guides, about 5 inches high, and the width of the guides. Fill the rectangle with a blue-to-white linear gradient using the blue color shown.

(2) Create the following angled Guides for a perspective grid:

* Vertical location 6⁹⁄₁₆ inches, angle 5 degrees
* Vertical location 6⅞ inches, angle 7 degrees
* Vertical location 7¹¹⁄₁₆ inches, angle 10 degrees

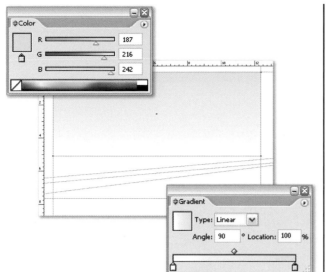

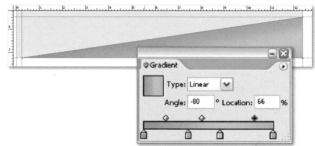

5 With the Pen tool, draw a closed path triangle using the bottom angled Guide to define the size of the triangle. Apply a linear gradient fill at a –80% angle with four color stops:

* Location: 0%, R=140, G=140, B=140
* Location: 35%, R=160, G=160, B=160
* Location: 60%, R=190, G=190, B=190
* Location: 100%, R=165, G=165, B=165

Set all the midpoint diamonds to 50%, except the last (third) one, which you set to 66%.

4 Use the area defined by the Guides to draw a gray-filled rectangle about 2½ inches high. Define the gray as shown.

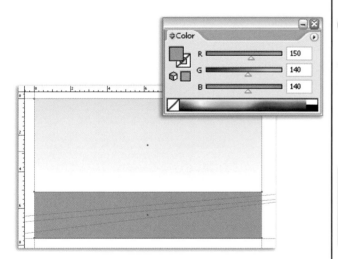

6 Use the Pen tool to draw the next strip of freeway as shown. Use five anchors—one for each corner, and create one anchor about midway on the top of the shape. Tweak the control point handle of that fifth anchor to bend the top path so that at the left edge of the Guides, the width of the strip is the distance from the bottom horizontal Guide to the second angled Guide; but on the right edge, the top-right corner anchor is almost at the *first* guide.

TIP

Distorting the perspective on this strip contributes to the feeling of stress, speed, and blur you're aiming for.

7 Use the middle angled Guide to draw the next strip of freeway as shown. As with the previous strip, tweak the anchors a bit (as shown). The point of all this is to make a linear blend which appears to "flare" out.

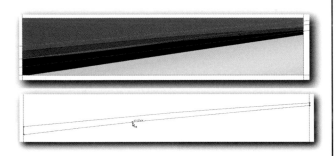

8 Complete the freeway strips by adding one that slightly overlaps the other two strips. Use a fifth anchor (in addition to the four corner anchors) on the bottom path to conform this strip to the same intensified perspective warp.

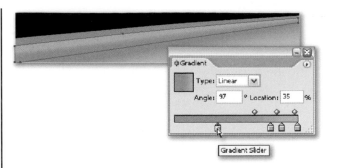

9 Apply a 97% angle, linear gradient fill to the middle freeway strip:

* Left gradient stop location: 35%. R=140, G=140, B=140
* Second from left gradient stop location: 75%. R=165, G=165, B=165
* Third from left gradient stop location: 85%. R=170, G=170, B=170
* Right gradient stop location: 100%. R=175, G=175, B=175

Set the three midpoint diamonds (starting from left) at 70%, 60%, and 85%.

10 Apply a 95% angle, linear gradient fill to the top freeway strip:

* Left gradient stop location: 6%. R=150, G=150, B=150
* Second from left gradient stop location: 21%. R=165, G=165, B=165
* Right gradient stop location: 100%. R=205, G=205, B=205

Set the left midpoint diamond at 60%, and the right midpoint diamond at 50%.

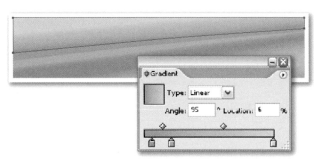

11 Prepare to create the diamond in the freeway by drawing a smaller diamond with a white fill and no stroke, enclosed by a larger diamond with a white fill but 0% opacity. You will blend an opaque white diamond into a fully transparent diamond in order to incrementally expose the gradient fill underneath the diamonds.

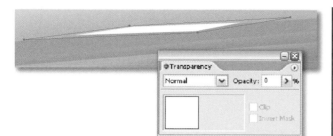

(13) Place a gray diamond in the middle of the blend.

(12) Generate a 20-step, step blend between the larger fully transparent diamond, and the smaller opaque white diamond. Click to select the Align to Page orientation icon.

California Drivers License Exam Note

In California, we have "carpool" lanes, which means that if you find one (or sometimes two) other person, you can whiz through traffic at rush hour in a separate lane. Of course that would mean two or more people in one car, which is a cultural issue out here and rarely happens. On the other hand, drivers are very creative using dummies, hats on sticks, and other forms of pretending to have a passenger in their car. These "carpool" lanes are designated with diamonds.

(14) Use the same technique to create a 20-step, step blend between a small white oval, and a larger fully transparent one to represent a lane divider dash (the broken-line lane dividers that are legal to change lanes through) from a high-speed perspective.

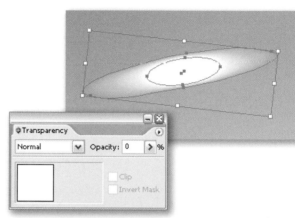

NOTE

You cannot generate a smooth blend between a 100-percent opaque shape and a path with transparency. You can only generate a step blend.

In the next step, you complete the process of creating white and yellow lane lines with a transparent step blend, with the foreground end of the lane stripes flaring out and blurring, thus keeping the speed effect consistent.

15 As a finishing touch, add more lane divider dashes. For an extra finishing touch, add or enhance lane dividers, and add a yellow solid-line ("do not cross") lane divider.

Highway Posts Lookin' Like a Picket Fence

In the previous task, you created the freeway background for this set of projects. Before you place a speeding vehicle in the illustration, you will create a few more elements that both stand alone as allusion to speed, and fit together into the cumulative project.

In this task, you create a freeway sign, as seen from the perspective of a vehicle being chased down the freeway at 120 mph.

(1) Draw a rectangle 6 inches high and ⅛ inches wide.

(2) Rotate the rectangle –5 degrees. To engage the Rotate tool, press the R key, and click at the base of the rectangle to define a rotation pivot point. Drag on the top of the rectangle to rotate it clockwise. Use the Info palette to know when the rotation is –5 degrees.

(3) Fill the rectangle with a –5% linear gradient with three color stops:

- Location: 0%. R=164, G=161, B=155
- Location: 30%. R=255, G=255, B=255 (white)
- Location: 100%. R=164, G=161, B=155

Set the first midpoint diamond to 60%, and the second (right) midpoint diamond to 50%.

NOTE

The red, green, and blue values for the gray in Step 3 create a slightly off-gray. Pure gray RGB mixes use the same value for all three colors. From an artistic point of view, grays made from combining colors are richer and more natural than grays made from black and white. You use this off-gray mix in many of the remaining tasks in this chapter.

anchor

Navigator ⬦Info
+ X : 4.2125 in
  Y : 8.4931 in
⌔ : -4.954°

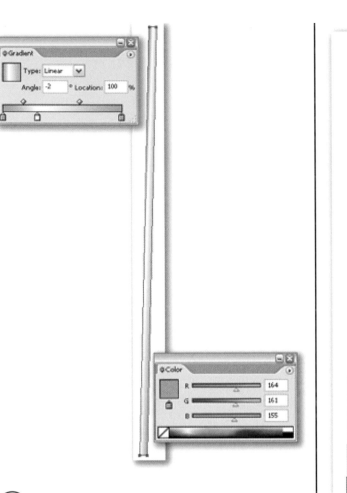

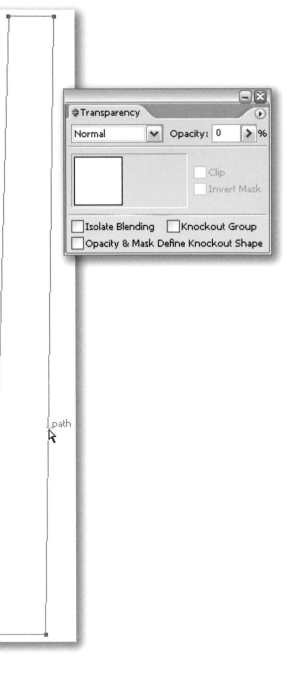

④ Draw a rectangle the same height as the pole (6 inches), and about a half inch wide. Apply no stroke, and a white (or any color) fill with 0% Opacity (from the Transparency palette).

NOTE

I won't point this out each time, but one more time will probably be helpful . . . you're preparing to blend a colored fill (in this case gray) into a completely transparent fill. The result is a transparent fill that allows incrementally more of the background gradient fills to show through contributing to the "from a speeding vehicle" effect you're going for in the whole illustration.

5 Copy the pole, and apply the same fill that you applied to the original pole (R=164, G=161, B=155). Place the copy in front of the transparent rectangle, slightly to the left of the horizontal center of the rectangle.

6 Assign 75% Opacity to the dark gray pole using the Transparency palette.

7 Apply a 20-step, aligned-to-the-page step blend between the copy of the pole and the ½-inch wide rectangle. (Press W for the Blend tool and click once on the pole and then the rectangle.)

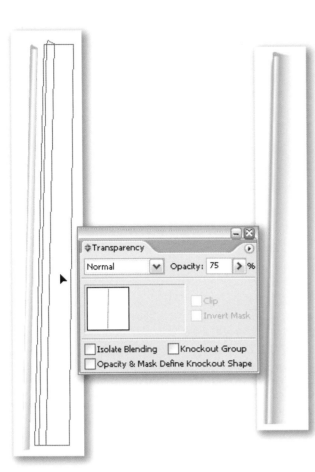

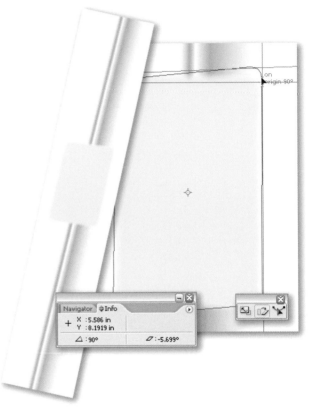

8 Using the Rounded Rectangle tool, draw a sign shape about 1.2 inches high, and about ¾ inch wide. Apply a yellow fill.

9 Use the Shear tool (really the Skew tool, but Adobe calls it the Shear tool in documentation) to *skew* the rounded rectangle about 2 degrees.

10 Duplicate the yellow sign, and assign a darker yellow fill (R=255, G=210, B=21).

Bug

Illustrator is supposed to allow you to edit either element of a blend, and when you edit one blended object, the generated blend is supposed to adjust automatically. That doesn't always work when you edit blended objects with different opacities. In particular it doesn't always work right with blends that involve one object with 100% transparency.

If you decide to tweak a blend that includes a transparent object, it's best to release the blend and ungroup the objects and start over. If you don't, you'll find that the changes don't update properly and you don't get correct info in the Transparency palette when you edit blended objects after you generate the blend.

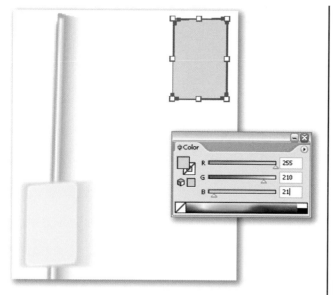

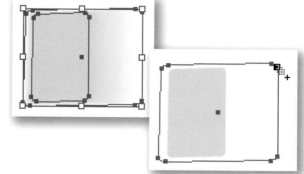

13 Generate a 20-step, page-aligned step blend between the transparent sign and the darkened sign.

14 Select the original sign shape. Choose Effect ➪ Stylize ➪ Feather and apply about a .12 inch feather effect.

11 Duplicate the darker (copy of the) sign. Use the bounding box to stretch it so the width is about 1½ inches and the height is about 1¾ inches.

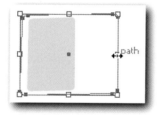

12 Assign 0% Opacity to the enlarged copy of the sign.

Move the blended signs behind the original sign, and you're done.

Task 29 shows you how to add a speed limit (like that matters!) to the sign.

Fly By Type

In Task 28, you created a blurred freeway sign as seen from a vehicle speeding past. You applied a step blend between an opaque and transparent version of the sign for a unique motion blur effect.

Here, you will apply some of the same "flying past" look to type so that the numbers on the sign mesh with the sign itself. First, you draw closed paths around the perimeter of the sign, with a line dividing the sign about one-third of the way down. Then, you painstakingly add each individual letter.

With all these elements, you apply similar motion blur effects created by blending opaque paths with transparent paths to gradually reveal underlying objects.

1 Use the Rectangle tool to draw a rectangle inside the yellow sign. Apply a 3-point black stroke and no fill.

2 With the rectangle selected, choose Filter ⇨ Stylize ⇨ Round Corners. Use the Round Corners dialog box (with the Preview checkbox selected) to apply slightly rounded corners—something like a radius of 1 inch—to the rectangle.

3 Use the Line tool to draw a 3-point, black horizontal line across the rectangle about one-third of the distance from the top of the (now rounded) rectangle.

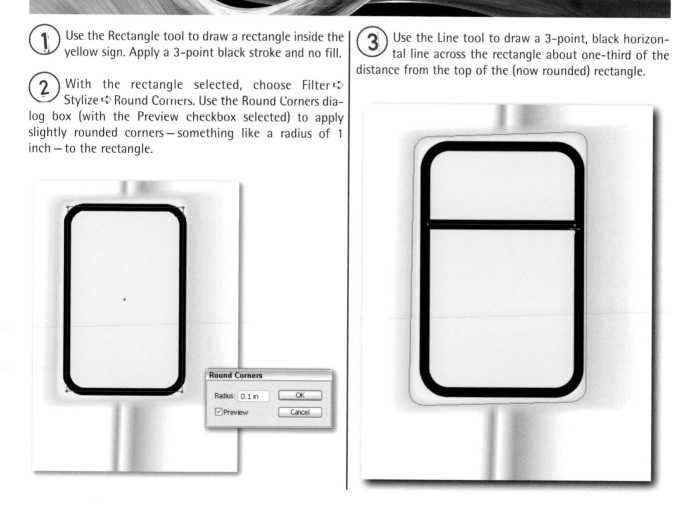

Round Corners

Radius: 0.1 in   OK
☑ Preview   Cancel

4 With both the rounded rectangle and the line selected, choose Object ⇨ Path ⇨ Outline Stroke to convert the paths to objects with fills.

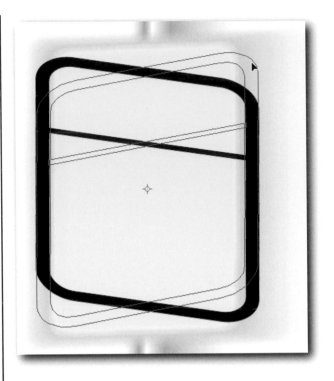

5 Select both paths, and use the Add tool in the Pathfinder palette to combine them.

TIP

The combined paths form a compound path that functions as a window over the sign — revealing the yellow underneath.

6 With the path still selected, use the Shear (Skew) tool to skew the new paths to match the skew of the sign.

7 Apply 75% Opacity to the paths in the Transparency palette.

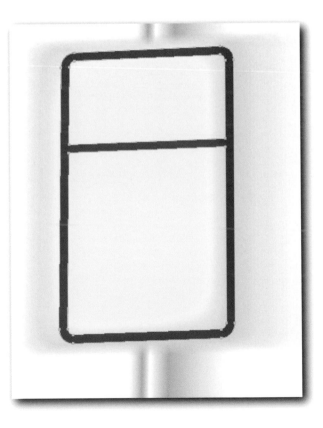

chapter 6 • blends on speed

8 Generate a blend for the outline paths by duplicating and then stretching the copied path to create a slightly wider version of the paths. Apply a black fill with no opacity to the copy, and create a 20-step, step blend between the two paths.

9 Create the first numeral for the sign, 3.

TIP

Click with the Type tool (press T to select it) and type **3**. From the Type palette (Command/Ctrl+T), choose Myriad 36-point bold font.

10 Convert the type to an outline. (Select the number with the Selection tool, and press Shift+Command/Ctrl+O.)

11 Copy the *3* (now a path) and paste in back. Stretch the copy horizontally about 20 percent using the bounding box.

(12) Apply a yellow fill with 0% opacity to the copied, horizontally stretched *3*.

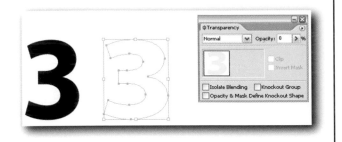

(13) Place the stretched *3* behind the original *3*, and generate a 20-step, page-aligned step blend between the two 3s.

(14) Place the blended 3 on top of the sign; it's the beginning of 30 (as in 30 mph).

(15) Create additional blended letters for the sign.

16 If you want, you can begin to composite all the tasks in this chapter by copying the sign on top of the freeway you created in Task 27.

Out-of-Control VW Minibus

Back in the day, we would trek across the country in VW Minibuses that would hold just about anything, but only went 60 miles per hour floored. And that was downhill.

In this task, you use the trick of using blends to convey motion one last time. This time, you'll use a variation of this technique to put some motion into Illustrator CS2's cute Minibus.

① Either working with the background you created in the past two tasks . . . or not . . . place the Minibus symbol from the Retro Symbols palette. You can display the Retro Symbols palette by choosing Window ⇨ Symbol Libraries ⇨ Retro. Drag the Minibus symbol out of the palette onto the artboard.

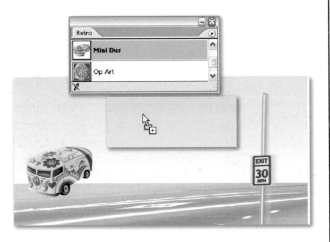

② With the Minibus selected, click on the upper-right bounding box handle with the Skew (Shear) tool. Drag down to align the Minibus with your background.

③ Select the skewed bus with the Selection tool, and adjust scaling and rotation using the bounding box.

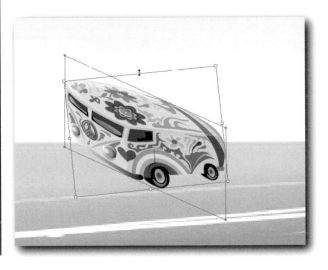

chapter 6 ● blends on speed

④ Option/Alt+drag the Minibus to create a copy.

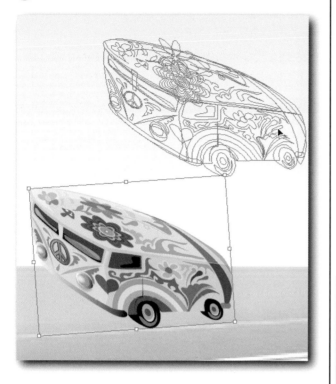

⑤ With the copy of the Minibus selected, choose Object ⇨ Expand to transform the symbol into a set of paths that can have Pathfinder effects applied.

NOTE

Select both the Object and Fill checkboxes in the Expand dialog box before you click OK. You are expanding a symbol *instance* so that it becomes an actual, editable path. Until you expand the symbol instance, you are constrained to essentially manipulating a copy of the saved symbol.

⑥ Option/Alt-click on the Add tool in the Pathfinder palette to convert the copy of the Minibus to a single closed path.

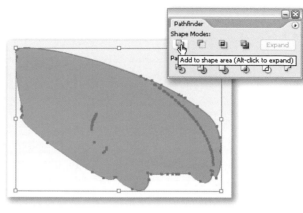

TIP

When adding shapes with the Pathfinder Add tool, you sometimes generate extra artifacts (junk paths—stuff you don't want). If that happens here, select everything, and switch to Outline view. In Outline view, Shift-click on the main shape that you want to keep (Shift-click deselects that shape). With the junk (artifact paths) selected, press the Delete key to remove the artifacts.

⑦ Apply a white fill (and no stroke) to the copy of the Minibus. Place the copy of the Minibus "a ways" behind the original Minibus. The greater the distance, the crazier the blend effect.

8 Apply 0% Opacity to the white Minibus in the Transparency palette.

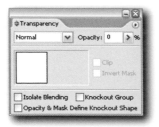

9 Create a 20-step, aligned-to-path step blend between the two vehicles.

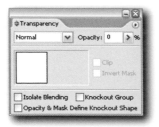

NOTE

Set blend options by choosing Object ⇨ Blend ⇨ Options. Press W for the Blend tool, and click on the colored Minibus, and then the white one.

10 You probably need to select the original Minibus with the Direct Selection tool. Control/right-click on the original bus, and choose Arrange ⇨ Bring to Front from the context menu.

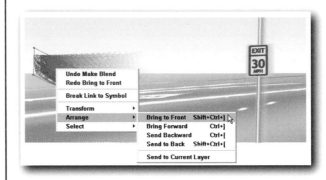

11 To touch up, you can tweak the control point handles on either end of the blend spine to add curvature to the motion blur.

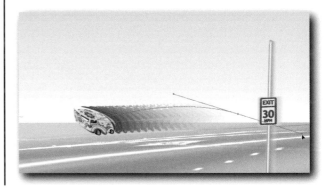

12 Finally, adjust the location of the blend against your background. Consider psychadelicizing the background by adding a gradient fill behind the speeding Minibus.

Keep this file open (go ahead and save it). You use it in the final task in this chapter.

Blur

In Task 30, you created a motion blur effect between the original Minibus and its ghostly (transparent) clone. You can enhance the blur impact by applying effects to both the blur and the original Minibus itself.

You can either apply these steps to the motion blur you created in Task 30, or, you can apply some of them to the Minibus symbol without going through the fun of creating the blur in Task 31. But don't — this will work better if you do Task 30 first.

1 With the whole blend selected, choose Darken from the Transparency palette pull-down menu.

2 Select just the original Minibus. With the original Minibus selected, choose Effect ➪ Stylize ➪ Feather. Set Feather Radius to about .1 (¹⁄₁₀) inch.

3 Select the (transparent) copy of the Minibus with the Direct Selection tool. Choose Effect ➪ Blur ➪ Gaussian Blur to apply a blur that will fade between the original and the invisible Minibus. Set the Blur Radius at 20 pixels.

4 For touchup, use the Appearance palette to tweak the effects applied to either the original or the copy of the Minibus. Here's the finished image.

illegal wheels

This chapter completes a trilogy of sorts. Chapter 5 explores some crazy stuff you can do with step blends. Chapter 6 is built around much more subtle blends. In this chapter, I'm heading in a different direction. Early digital illustrators (in the pre-gradient, pre-transparency, pre-blend days) had to create depth by layering individual flat colors. There are still realms of digital design where stacking up flat colors is the only way to achieve depth. For instance, until recently most textile processes didn't support gradients or blends.

Although Illustrator CS2 (and its predecessors) allows illustrators to save hours and hours of work by generating blends and gradients, there is still a value to creating depth by stacking individual flat colors. There is more life, more intensity, and a certain surrealism that can be achieved only by painstakingly building up color paths on a photo. At the other end of the hard-work/no-work spectrum, the last task in this chapter shows how fun and easy it can be to create a motion-blurred truck from a photo in five or six steps.

Hot Exhaust Pipe

Illustrator Chris Nielson does some spectacular work with cars, motorcycles, and chrome. You can see (and purchase!) some of his work at http://home.comcast.net/~carartwork. Chris does his magic with an amazing lack of effects. His "trick" is a lot of hard work — painstakingly tracing bitmaps brought into Illustrator as template layers.

"As for any time-saving tricks," Chris told me, "The only thing I can say is that I use the Pathfinder palette . . . *a lot*!!!" I'll break that down by deconstructing the exhaust pipe that is part of a larger Ducati motorcycle project of Chris's. You can replicate this project by using the JPEG photo file of the Ducati at www.davidkarlins.com/illustrator.

1 Create a new Illustrator file, and choose File ⇨ Place to open the Place dialog box. Navigate to a car photo (feel free to use Chris's at www.davidkarlins.com/illustrator). In the Place dialog box, select the Template checkbox to place the photo in a locked (template) layer and click Place to create the background layer for your illustration.

2 Name the non-template layer in your document for the part you are going to create. This layer is editable (as opposed to the locked template layer).

Layering?

For the most part, in this book, I've avoided discussing how you might (or might not) organize your projects into layers. That's not because layers are not useful or expedient. Large complex projects are much more easily managed by organizing different elements into layers that can be hidden or locked to facilitate focusing on separate sections of the project.

I'm avoiding discussion of layers because most of the projects in this book are bite-sized and manageable. And, because I'm avoiding the kinds of Illustrator workflow issues that you'll find explored in detail in books like the *Illustrator CS 2 Bible*.

On the other hand, if your frame of reference is a raster editor like Photoshop, you'll find layers are not quite as indispensable in Illustrator. That's because Illustrator paths are selectable, discrete objects (as opposed to that mass of pixelated stuff you deal with in Photoshop), layers generally don't play the same decisive role in Illustrator that they do in bitmap editing programs.

However, for complex tracing projects like this one, the sheer volume of paths makes it insane to try to manage the file without organizing different parts of — in this case the motorcycle — into layers.

3 Use the Zoom tool to create the largest possible picture of the entire exhaust pipe (or, whatever part it is you are working on first). Select the layer you named for this part.

(4) Working from the outside in, draw an ellipse around the circumference of the end of the exhaust pipe. Apply no fill and no stroke.

TIP

Without a stroke, you might have trouble locating this path when it is deselected. For a quick solution, toggle over to Outline view to locate and select the path when necessary. Or, you could apply a stroke for now — just to make it easier to find the path — and then remove the stroke later.

(5) Select the shape you drew by outlining the part. Copy it, and lock the original (Command/Ctrl+2). Paste the copy in front of the original.

TIP

The original is now safely locked. You might want to use it later as a transparency overlay, or to start from scratch if you need the larger shape again. You are about to chop this piece into many, many paths, and reconstructing it will be a hassle.

(6) Draw another ellipse inside the original ellipse to mark the inside of the exhaust pipe. Select both ellipses, and click the Divide tool in the Pathfinder palette to "cut out" the smaller circle.

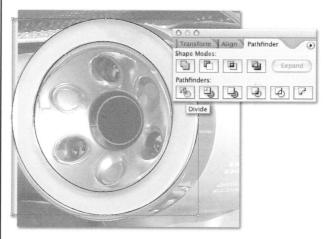

(7) As promised, now comes the tedious part. One by one, draw paths (with no fill or stroke) with the Pen tool, and select both the new path and the larger path that it falls within. With both paths selected, click the Divide tool in the Pathfinder palette to generate new paths.

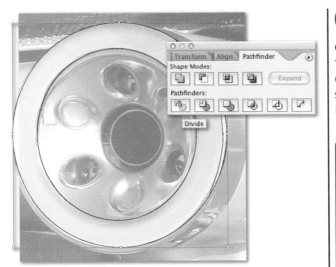

9 One technique for assigning colors to the multitude of paths is to use the Eyedropper tool (I) to select colors for the Color palette. With a closed path selected use the Eyedropper tool to select a color from the corresponding part of the photo. Then, with the color selected, intensify the coloring using the sliders in the RGB color palette. For instance, you can tint grays with more blue.

TIP

You can adjust the tint of a hue by holding down the Shift key as you drag on a slider in the RGB Color palette. Holding down the Shift key moves all three colors equally. . This works *unless* you are dragging the sliders to the left and one channel is at 255 or one is at 0.

8 Several hours later . . . you will have drawn about a hundred paths. (I was kidding about the hours, but not the 100.) The more paths you create, the more control you have over the final coloring.

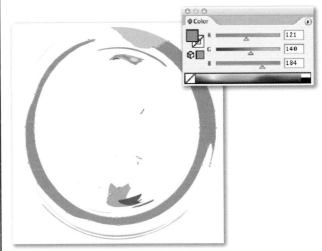

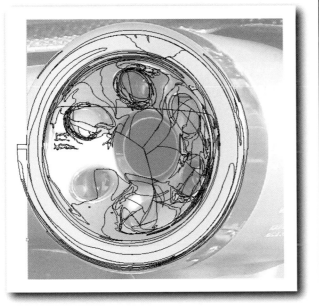

10 Continue applying colors, one by one, to each path in the illustration. Use your original photo for guidance, and then crank up the colors, adding high contrast to the original colors for more intensity.

11 The final exhaust pipe contains no gradient fills, providing a surreal, unique blend of colors.

Paint by Numbers

Some details in photo-based artwork have to be created from scratch. For instance, you might elect not to include your own license plate numbers when vectorizing your car. Chris Nielsen's Ducati project introduced in Task 32 includes license plate numbers that could not simply be traced. It's instructive and interesting to see how he created the numbers, maintaining the same coloring logic he uses on the bike engine and other parts.

The approaches in this task are useful for enhancing and altering a photo-based illustration, *or* for creating a glossy paint look that can be used in any set of characters in any illustration.

As with Task 32, the basic approach you use here is to build dimension by creating larger shapes first and then carving them up into smaller paths, or by layering smaller shapes on top of larger shapes.

(1) Create the number *20* in broad strokes, using a filled-in ellipse for the zero. Apply no stroke to the paths, but use R=45, B=90, and G=160 as a fill for both numbers.

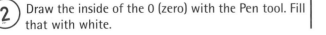

(2) Draw the inside of the 0 (zero) with the Pen tool. Fill that with white.

3 Add purple (use R=173, B=132, G=186) highlights to the upper-left sides of the numbers.

4 Use many shades of gray for shadowing on the lower and right side of each section of each number.

5 Enhance the shading with nearly black stripes on the lower-left sides of paths, and some additional purple shading.

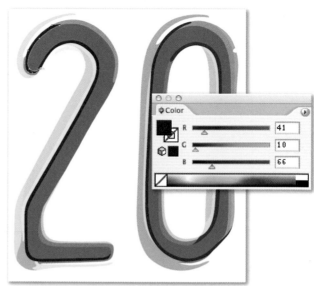

6 The final numbers are an interesting stand-alone project. Or, you can add more numbers and create a license plate (see the next page).

EZ Wheels

Having exposed you to a mind-numbingly tedious, if ultimately rewarding method for vectorizing a vehicle, it's only fair to examine the easy way. Just how good is Illustrator CS2's Live Trace feature? Awfully good.

In this task, I demonstrate how clean and sharp a vector you can create using the Live Trace tool. After the Live Trace, of course, you can apply all the effects you wish to the generated vectors.

1 Define (or make sure you have defined) an RGB color space (choose File ⇨ Document color Mode ⇨ RGB File).

NOTE

More effects are available in RGB color mode.

2 Get your hands on a truck photo. You can download this JPEG from www.illustratorgonewild.com.

3 Place the truck raster file. (Choose File ⇨ Place, and deselect Link in the Place dialog box.) This time, do *not* select the Template checkbox. You aren't using this raster photo file as a traceable template layer; you are going to convert it to a vector.

4 With your placed truck raster image selected and the Control palette displayed, click Live Trace in the Control palette. From the presets popup, choose Photo Low Fidelity.

5 In the Preview Different Views of the Raster Image popup in the Control palette, choose No Image. In the Preview Different Views of the Vector Result popup, choose Tracing Result. Click Expand to generate a vector from the photo.

6 Double-click on the rectangle around the truck to select both the rectangle, and the background shape. Press the Delete key to delete both the box and the background around the truck.

7 That's it? No, you can edit any of the vectors. Delete the vectors identifying the truck brand to keep the illustration generic. Touch up the generated trace as needed. Now you can apply any vector effect you want to the truck. Start with feathering, with a .13-inch radius (choose Effect ⇨ Stylize ⇨ Feather).

Feather	
Feather Radius: ⊕ 0.13 in	OK
☐ Preview	Cancel

8 Pile on another effect — they're free! Apply a Gaussian Blur (with the truck selected, choose Effect ⇨ Blur ⇨ Gaussian Blur). Set the radius at about 4 pixels.

post big-bang type

I recently attended the "Belles Lettres: The Art of Typography" exhibit at San Francisco Museum of Modern Art and saw some wild and crazy stuff with letters. Great show. My only issue with the work there is that, to me, if you're going to do graphic design with letters, you should be able to read something. Just an opinion – worth about 2 cents.

In this chapter, you do crazy stuff with type, but you produce projects that are readable. You wrap type around a 3D object. You apply opacity masking to type. You learn a couple different techniques for filling and outlining graffiti. And, if after all that you're still not locked up, I show you how to make it look like your graffiti is spray-painted on a brick wall.

Global Bang!

In Chapter 1, I focused on Illustrator CS2's 3D mapping effects, including the ability to map a symbol onto a 3D object.

In this task, you will return to the concept of using outlined type as a mappable symbol on a 3D effect. By mapping text on a globe, you achieve an extruded effect with more of a spherical look than you could achieve with simple extrusion.

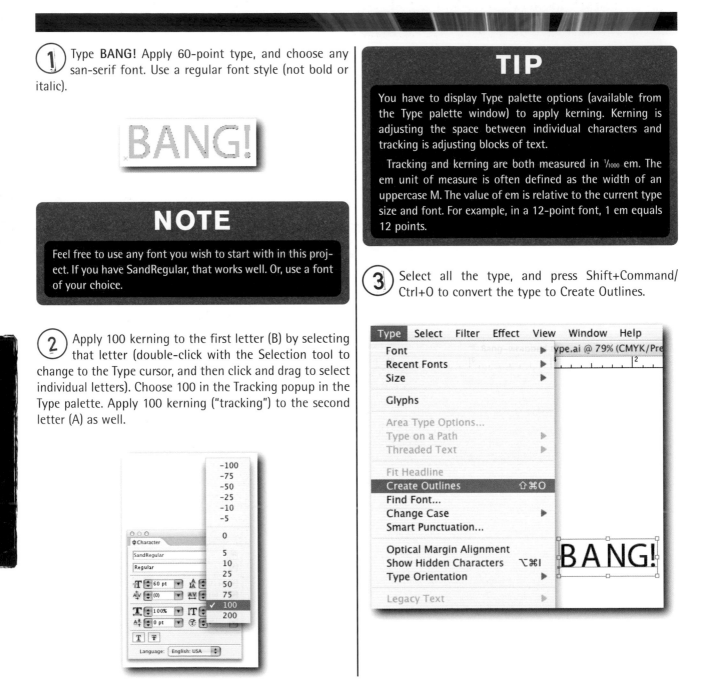

① Type **BANG!** Apply 60-point type, and choose any san-serif font. Use a regular font style (not bold or italic).

NOTE

Feel free to use any font you wish to start with in this project. If you have SandRegular, that works well. Or, use a font of your choice.

② Apply 100 kerning to the first letter (B) by selecting that letter (double-click with the Selection tool to change to the Type cursor, and then click and drag to select individual letters). Choose 100 in the Tracking popup in the Type palette. Apply 100 kerning ("tracking") to the second letter (A) as well.

TIP

You have to display Type palette options (available from the Type palette window) to apply kerning. Kerning is adjusting the space between individual characters and tracking is adjusting blocks of text.

Tracking and kerning are both measured in $\frac{1}{1000}$ em. The em unit of measure is often defined as the width of an uppercase M. The value of em is relative to the current type size and font. For example, in a 12-point font, 1 em equals 12 points.

③ Select all the type, and press Shift+Command/Ctrl+O to convert the type to Create Outlines.

CAUTION

Maybe it's not such a hot idea to use keyboard shortcuts here. They work only if you select the type *with the Selection tool*. I always forget to switch to the Selection key before administering keyboard shortcuts, and end up typing presumed keyboard shortcuts right into a text box as type. It's safer to choose Type ➪ Convert to Outlines from the menu.

④ With the new, outlined path selected, clean up superfluous paths by choosing Object ➪ Path ➪ Simplify. In the Simplify dialog box, set the Angle Threshold to 0 (zero), and the Curve Precision slider to 80%. Click OK. The appearance of the generated outline paths does not change much. But the number of anchors is greatly reduced, which makes the paths easier to work with when applying effects. Simplifying the paths pays off even more in the next task, when you map this text on a 3D object.

⑤ Select Filter ➪ Distort ➪ Pucker & Bloat, and apply a –16% Pucker to the selected paths.

⑥ Drag the BANG! paths into the Symbol palette to save the paths as a symbol for 3D mapping. Name the symbol **BANG**.

⑦ Draw a semicircle with a diameter of about 2.5 inches. Apply no stroke, and any fill to the semicircle. One quick way is to draw a circle, and use the Direct Selection tool to delete one of the generated four anchors.

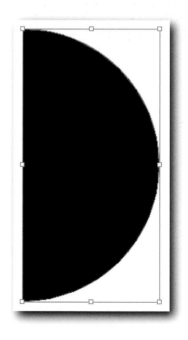

8 With the semicircle selected, choose Effect ⇨ 3D ⇨ Revolve. Define 20% rotation on the X-axis, and no (zero) rotation on the Y and Z axes. Set Perspective to 120 degrees, and set the Revolve Angle to 360 degrees. Select Wireframe from the Surface popup.

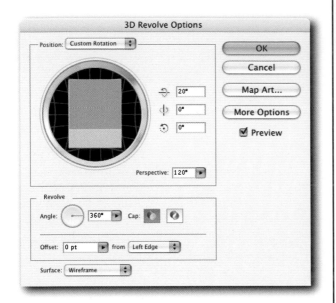

9 Click the Map Art button in the 3D Revolve dialog box. Because you generated a globe from a semicircle with no stroke, there will be only one mappable surface. From the Symbol popup, choose the BANG symbol. Click the Preview checkbox, and rely on the preview generated on the artboard to locate the BANG symbol. After you locate the symbol, click OK twice to generate the 3D mapped text.

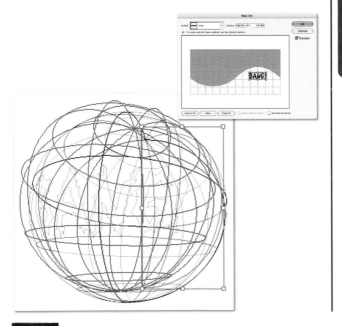

TIP

If you find the result of your mapping isn't quite right, view the Appearance palette, and with the generated 3D effect selected, double-click the effect in the Appearance palette to reopen the 3D Revolve dialog box. Don't try accessing your existing effect from the Effect menu; that allows you to add only *another* instance of this (or another) effect.

10 With the 3D effect selected, choose Object ⇨ Expand Appearance. Clean up the text by deleting the wireframe.

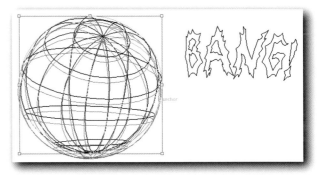

TIP

To facilitate deleting the wireframe, start by performing multiple ungroups until the generated paths are completely ungrouped. Use the Direct Selection tool (A) to select the paths remaining from the wireframe and delete them.

Another approach is to select the type and the outer circle and lock these paths (Command/Ctrl+2). Then delete remaining wireframes all at once.

11 Duplicate the type, and place a scaled copy about half the size of the original behind and slightly below the original so that the original covers about half of the copy.

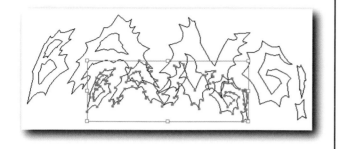

12 Apply different fills and strokes to each character (and be sure to use *different* fills and strokes for the large and small version of each character). Generate smooth blends between the large and small versions of each character. (Generate separate blends between the top and bottom of the exclamation mark; these are two separate paths.) Move objects to the back as necessary.

13 Expand the blend (Object ⇨ Blend ⇨ Expand). Select the faces of the larger characters, and apply radial gradient blends to each one.

14 This next step might be a bit tedious for those of you who have jobs to get to tomorrow, but you can add plenty to the project by using the Pen tool and Pathfinder to draw (and Divide — using the Pathfinder Divide tool) individual paths along the blend lines. Apply linear gradient fills to each of the resulting paths.

15 Finish off the project by applying linear gradient fills to all the paths created from the blend lines, and place the whole project against a dark, contrasting background. Move letters in front of or behind other letters as necessary to complete the illustration.

Shanghai Type

Using letters as clipping masks is both old hat, and incredible fun. For this task, you put a new *warp* (literally) into an old trick and create an unusual text clipping mask.

If you want to follow my project exactly, "borrow" the Shanghai.jpg photo at www.illustratorgonewild.com. Or, substitute your own travel photo (and alter my instructions to create text with the name of your locale). If you use Shanghai.jpg, download it now and remember where you saved it.

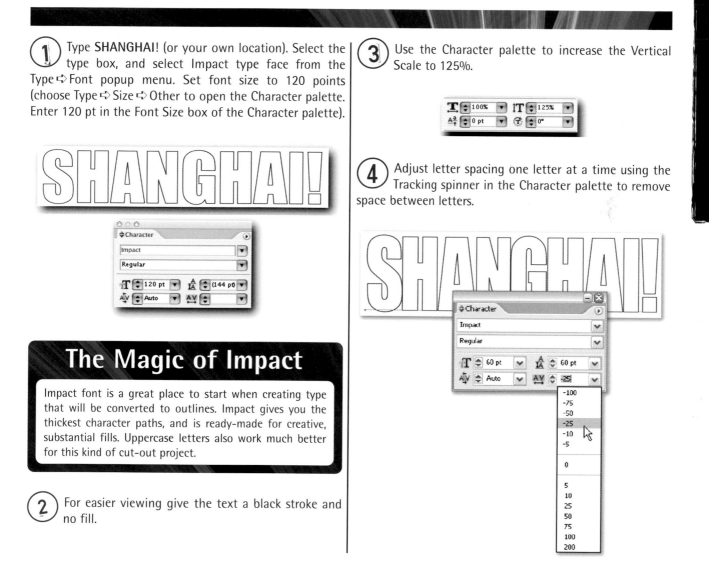

1. Type **SHANGHAI!** (or your own location). Select the type box, and select Impact type face from the Type ⇨ Font popup menu. Set font size to 120 points (choose Type ⇨ Size ⇨ Other to open the Character palette. Enter 120 pt in the Font Size box of the Character palette).

The Magic of Impact

Impact font is a great place to start when creating type that will be converted to outlines. Impact gives you the thickest character paths, and is ready-made for creative, substantial fills. Uppercase letters also work much better for this kind of cut-out project.

2. For easier viewing give the text a black stroke and no fill.

3. Use the Character palette to increase the Vertical Scale to 125%.

4. Adjust letter spacing one letter at a time using the Tracking spinner in the Character palette to remove space between letters.

5 After tuning up the type tracking, select the whole text box, and choose Object ⇨ Envelope Distort ⇨ Make With Warp. From the Style popup in the Warp Options dialog box, choose Rise. Set Bend to 50, Horizontal to –50, and Vertical to 13. Click OK to apply the warp.

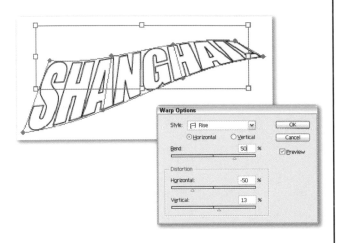

6 The warp is an effect. Expand the paths (to transform this into an object, not an effect) by selecting the warped type, and choosing Object ⇨ Expand.

7 Make the type a bit weirder by applying a little pucker. With the type selected, choose Filter ⇨ Distort ⇨ Pucker & Bloat. Set the slider in the Pucker & Bloat dialog box to –3 to define a slight pucker.

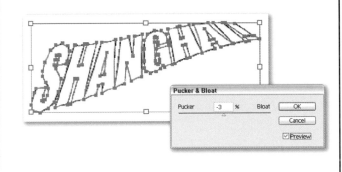

8 Use the Delete Anchor Point tool and touch up the outline by deleting unwanted anchors. Pay special attention to cleaning up the *S* and *G* in Shanghai, if you used my example.

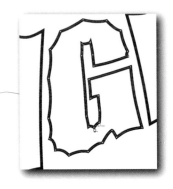

9 This step should not really be necessary, but both my PC and Mac versions of Illustrator CS2 require it before I can use the outlined type as a clipping mask. With (all) the type selected, choose Object ⇨ Compound Path ⇨ Make.

10 Select File ⇨ Place, and navigate to the Shanghai.jpg photo. Deselect the Link and Template checkboxes, and click OK to place the photo on the artboard.

⑪ Move the placed photo behind the type.

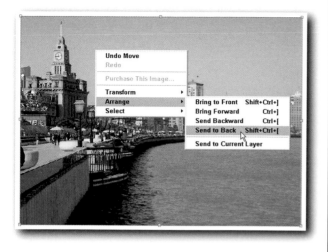

⑫ Locate the type over the photo in a place where you think you'll achieve an interesting effect using it as a clipping mask. Feel free to resize or reshape the text outlines. When you're happy with your placement (or ready to experiment), select both the text and the photo, and choose Object ⇨ Clipping Mask ⇨ Make.

⑬ Take full advantage of Command/Ctrl+Z to undo your initial attempt(s), and experiment until you get a nice clipped mask of the photo.

Chevy Type

In Task 36, you put a warp on the old text-as-clipping mask routine. In this task, you visit an entirely different way to use type as a clipping mask. This time, you apply gradient fills and drop shadows to the type — which by law you really shouldn't be able to do with a clipping mask. But rather than ruin the surprise, I'll let you follow the steps and see how to integrate effects into a type clipping mask.

For this project, I borrowed a car from Serge Timacheff, with whom I have co-authored a couple of books on digital photography. You can "borrow" Serge's photo from the book web site (www.illustratorgonewild.com).

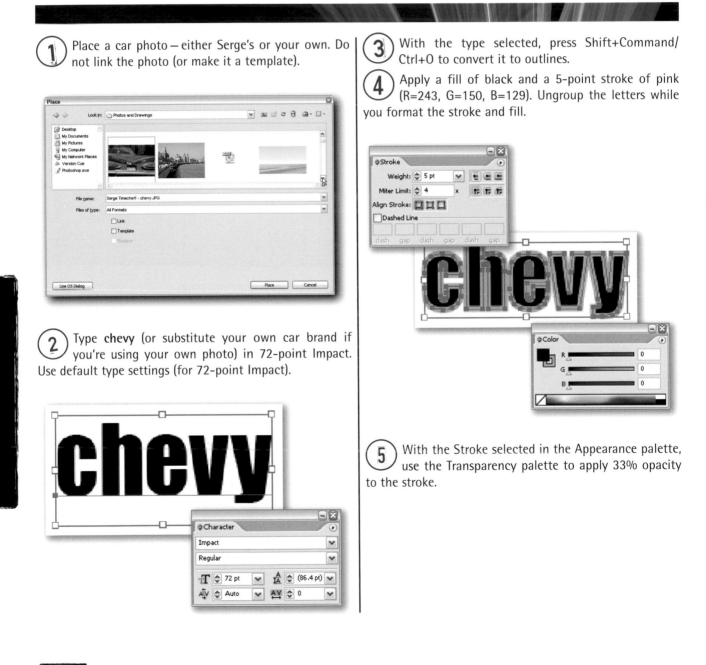

1 Place a car photo — either Serge's or your own. Do not link the photo (or make it a template).

2 Type **chevy** (or substitute your own car brand if you're using your own photo) in 72-point Impact. Use default type settings (for 72-point Impact).

3 With the type selected, press Shift+Command/ Ctrl+O to convert it to outlines.

4 Apply a fill of black and a 5-point stroke of pink (R=243, G=150, B=129). Ungroup the letters while you format the stroke and fill.

5 With the Stroke selected in the Appearance palette, use the Transparency palette to apply 33% opacity to the stroke.

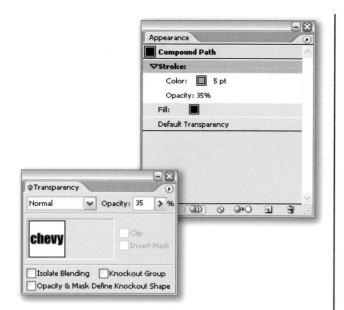

6 With all the outlined text selected, group the text. With the shape selected, choose Effect ➪ 3D ➪ Extrude & Bevel. Set X rotation at −18 degrees, Y rotation at −26 degrees, and Z rotation at 8 degrees. Set Extrude Depth to 50 points. Choose a Plastic Shading surface, and define a single light source in the upper right (this is the default setting).

CAUTION

You can get away with enlarging a placed photo *sometimes*. Remember, of course, that placed raster images are *not* scalable (like vector images). If your work is destined for print output, it is necessary to use a high-resolution photo (like 180 dpi or higher), and avoid enlarging it. If your illustration is for digital display, a 72 dpi photo will work fine, and you might get away with a bit of enlargement because after clipping, the details won't be important and some graininess is tolerable. Your vector text, on the other hand, is fully scalable.

7 Place the type on top of your car photo. Resize the type as necessary, and locate it on a good place to create what will be *something like* a clipping mask.

8 *Don't* get ready to use the type as a clipping mask. If you did that, you'd lose the impact of the gradient fill and the drop shadows, and simply fill the basic text object paths with pieces of the photo. Instead, select both the photo and the outlined text, and choose Make Opacity Mask from the Transparency palette.

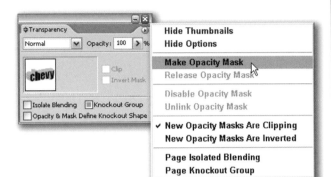

9 Select both the Inverse and Clip checkboxes in the Transparency palette.

10 Enhance the illustration with a gradient fill background to finish up the project.

Shanghai II

Another approach to creating the fun travel postcard look is to apply transparency masking to type. Transparency masking can be used with outlined type to create even more intriguing clipping masks. In this exercise, you apply one of the really groovy graphic type styles that ship with Illustrator CS2 and then use that souped-up type as a transparency mask.

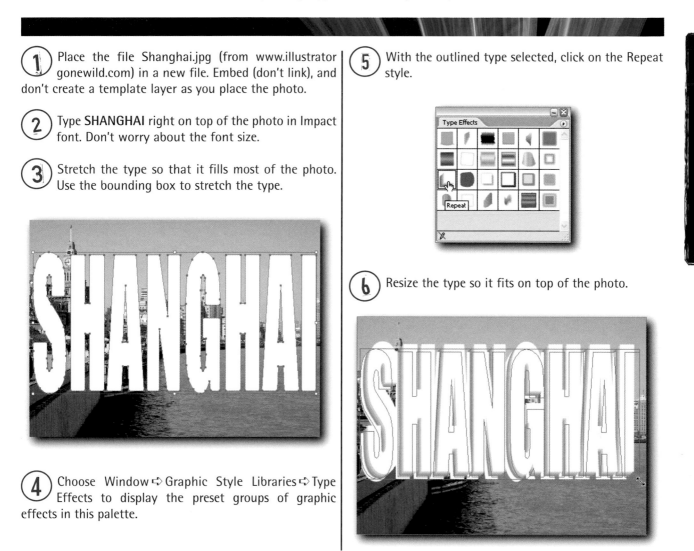

1 Place the file Shanghai.jpg (from www.illustrator gonewild.com) in a new file. Embed (don't link), and don't create a template layer as you place the photo.

2 Type **SHANGHAI** right on top of the photo in Impact font. Don't worry about the font size.

3 Stretch the type so that it fills most of the photo. Use the bounding box to stretch the type.

4 Choose Window ➪ Graphic Style Libraries ➪ Type Effects to display the preset groups of graphic effects in this palette.

5 With the outlined type selected, click on the Repeat style.

6 Resize the type so it fits on top of the photo.

7 Select both the outlined type and the photo. From the Transparency palette fly-out menu, choose Make Opacity Mask. Check only the Clip checkbox.

8 You can add a background to finalize the project, and rotate the type counterclockwise about 10 degrees for that tacky postcard look.

Digital Graffiti 1

Illustrator's ability to stack up multiple stroke and fill attributes on a single path is one of the more underrated elements of this Byzantine program. The basic concept is, one stroke, many stroke attributes. One fill, many fill attributes. For instance, you can stack up a thin black line, a thicker red line underneath it, and an even thicker yellow line . . . and they're all attributes of the *same* path.

Same thing with fills. You can stack a gradient on top of a color, and stick another gradient on top of the whole pile.

Multiple path attributes are defined in the Appearance palette, where they can be restacked, removed, or dragged over to the Graphic Styles palette for re-use. You'll do all that in this first of two graffiti projects.

① Use the Pen (or Pencil) tool to draw your favorite tag art. Draw closed paths. Set stroke width to .5 points, and mix up your fill colors. To create letters with holes, draw the shape and the holes, and then select the whole letter and press Command/Ctrl+8 or choose Object ⇨ Compound Path ⇨ Make.

② Complete a basic version of your tag, and select the path around one of the letters. (You can enhance the tag later, but stop after you create a basic version to enhance the paths — using the technique I walk you through in the next step.)

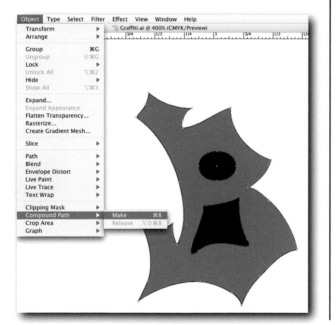

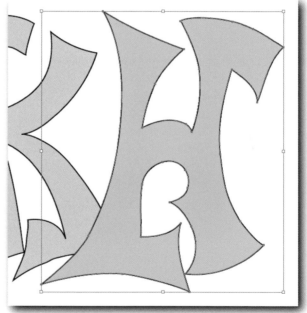

3 With the stroke of one of your letters (or tag characters) selected, view the Appearance palette. In the Appearance palette, select the stroke. From the Appearance menu, choose Add New Stroke.

5 Add a third, 8-point stroke under the second one in the Appearance palette. Make the third stroke red.

4 With the second stroke selected, choose 4 point in the Stroke palette. Assign a yellow stroke color to the selected (second) stroke.

TIP

As you can see, you can stack up strokes (and fills) in the Appearance palette. And, as you'll see shortly, you can save the whole set of graphic strokes and apply them as a graphic style.

6 Select the fill in the Appearance palette for your selected character. Choose Add New Fill from the Appearance palette menu.

7 Select the top fill in the Appearance palette, and apply a radial gradient to that fill by choosing a fill from the Gradient palette (or a Swatch palette) with the fill strip selected in the Appearance palette.

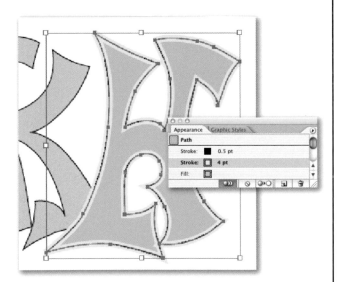

8 Continue to select the top fill in the Appearance palette. With the fill selected there, apply 25% opacity using the Transparency palette, and choose Multiply as the blending mode.

9 Drag the icon in the Appearance palette into the Graphic Style palette. Name the new graphic style **Graffiti**.

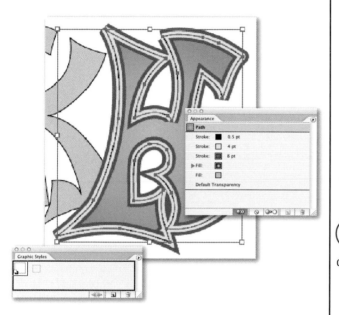

10 Select another letter in your tag. With the letter selected, click the Graffiti graphic style icon in the Graphic Styles palette to apply that style to the path. Apply the graphic style to all the paths in your tag.

11 Select the entire tag. Copy it, and paste it to the back of the existing tag. In the Appearance palette, delete the fills and strokes. Assign a black fill and black stroke to the copied tag. "Why?" you ask. You are creating a backing copy of the tag with a black outline to use for generating a blur. You won't see the outline now, but the black stroke will be useful in defining the color of the blur you create in the next step.

12 With the (hidden, underlying) tag selected, choose Effect ⇨ Blur ⇨ Gaussian Blur. In the Gaussian Blur dialog box, select a Radius of about 10 pixels.

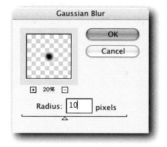

13 Because the Gaussian Blur is an effect, you can touch it up (make the radius larger or smaller) by double-clicking on the effect in the Appearance palette with the tag selected.

Digital Graffiti II

Here's another take on the graffiti that looks great on a wall. I was going to call it Physical Graffiti II, but I already burned my quota of Led Zeppelin disses in the last chapter.

For this version of graffiti type, you will ditch the interesting technique of applying multiple strokes and fills (from Task 39). Instead, you'll use a different approach to defining a fill and stroke for letters that will look better on a wall.

① As you did with the previous task, start out by using the Pen (or Pencil) tool to draw your favorite tag art with closed paths. As with Task 39, use compound paths for the holes in letters (such as the triangle in the letter *A*, the two "holes" in the letter *B*, and so on.

② Use the Stroke palette to align all strokes to inside and round join all the strokes.

③ Add fill and stroke colors of your choice to each character in your tag.

④ Using the Pen or Pencil tool, add decorative colored stroke squiggles.

Graffiti Wall

The graffiti you created in Task 40 goes great on a wall. So, here, you create that wall using pattern fill. The twist is that to achieve a real "painted on" look between the wall and your graffiti, you're going to put a semi-transparent wall *on top of* the lettering.

1 Set up the artboard for this project by defining grids every ¹⁄₁₆ of an inch. Choose Illustrator/Edit ➪ Preferences ➪ Guides and Grid. Set grid to 16 divisions per inch.

Preferences

Guides & Grid

Guides
Color: ▨ Cyan
Style: Lines

Grid
Color: Other...
Style: Lines
Gridline every: 1 in
Subdivisions: 16
☑ Grids In Back

OK
Cancel
Previous
Next

2 Select View ➪ Show Grid to display the grid you defined.

3 Turn on Snap to Grid (choose View ➪ Snap to Grid).

4 Use the Rounded Rectangle tool to make a brick. Apply these settings: Width: .75 in, Height: .25 in, Corner Radius: .3125 in).

Rounded Rectangle

Options
Width: 0.75 in
Height: 0.25 in
Corner Radius: 0.03125 in

OK
Cancel

5 Hold down the Option/Alt key, and drag the brick horizontally to create a vertically aligned copy located ¹⁄₁₆" (one grid segment) to the right of the original.

6 Select both bricks, and copy them ¹⁄₁₆ inch (one grid segment) below the existing rounded rectangles.

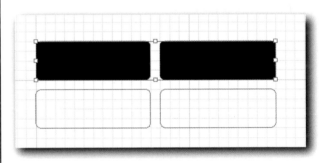

7 Re-arrange the bottom row of bricks so that *one* of the bricks is centered under the top bricks. Delete the left-over brick, as shown.

8 Use the Rectangle tool (not the Rounded Rectangle tool this time) to draw an unfilled rectangle ³⁄₁₆ inch wide and ¹⁰⁄₁₆ (⅝ inch, but the grids make it easier to think of it as ¹⁰⁄₁₆ inch) high. Align the rectangle *behind* the bricks as shown. Apply a gray fill to the backing rectangle using RGB settings of R=167, G=174, B=179.

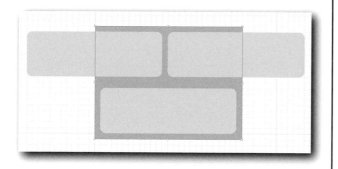

9 Draw a lot of tiny, random white-filled shapes (on top of all the other objects) within the area defined by the bottom rectangle. It's fine (and will create a more realistic texture) if a few of the white texture spots extend a bit beyond the edge of the rectangle.

TIP

For a better understanding of the art of creating non-stereotypical pattern fills (as well as the basic techniques involved), jump back to Chapter 2 and read some of the introductory notes and tips — especially the introduction to the entire Chapter 2.

10 Apply a gray fill to the three bricks using these RGB values: R=209, G=212, B=205. Select all the random little texture bits, and choose Overlay from the Transparency palette.

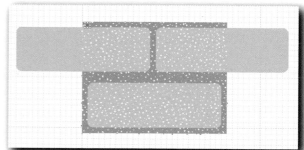

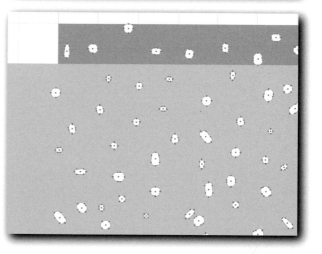

TIP

Select all the random texture bits by selecting one of them, and then choosing Select ⇨ Same ⇨ Fill Color. Because the random texture bits are the only white-filled objects in the file, you can grab them all in a hurry, and not select anything else.

(11) Apply a drop shadow to the bricks — but not by using the drop shadow effect. Instead, copy the three bricks, and paste them in back. Paste the second copy in back, and offset either copy slightly. Color both back bricks black. Apply 0% opacity to the offset brick, and define a ten-step, step blend between the opaque and the fully transparent black background brick.

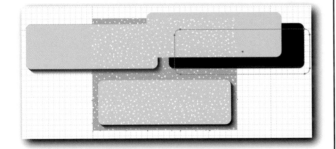

(12) Select the backing rectangle. Copy that rectangle, and paste it behind everything. Assign no stroke or fill to the copied rectangle.

(13) Drag everything to the Swatches palette. You'll use the content constrained by the rectangle as a repeating pattern fill.

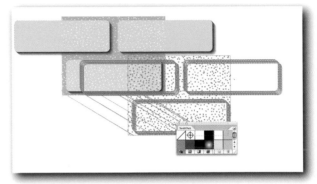

(14) Create a background rectangle (to become a wall) for the graffiti art. To do that, use the brick swatch you created in Step 13 to fill the rectangle (just click on the swatch).

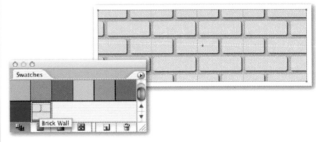

15) Place the graffiti from Task 40 on the wall. Move the wall on top of the graffiti (resize as necessary). With the rectangle selected, choose Multiply in the Transparency palette. By placing a transparency-applied wall *over* the type, you add dimension and texture to the graffiti.

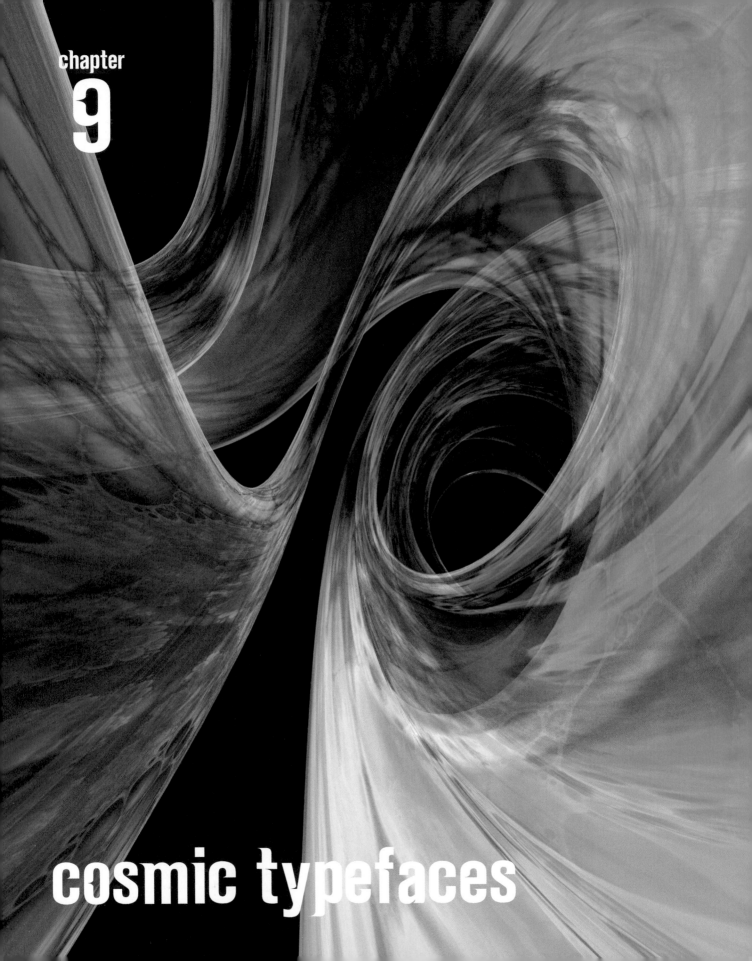

chapter

9

cosmic typefaces

In the previous chapter, I introduced you to some tricks and approaches for messing around with typefaces. In this chapter, you push the type envelope even farther.

The bloody Dracula type projects at the beginning of the chapter focus on some techniques for applying a high degree of distortion in a relatively uniform way to type. Each letter is handcrafted but at the same time appears to be part of a coherent (if deranged) font.

The other tasks here play around with 3D effects. Extruded type is the oldest trick in the . . . universe, but you find some new ways of playing with it in the Star Wars rip-off project. Last, but definitely not least, you revisit the spiral type tricks explored in the very first task in this book, but flip the spiral forward to create the oh-so-in-demand flushed-down-a-toilet look for your type.

Crystallized Type

There will always be a market for Dracula fonts. In this (and the following) task, I show you how to create a suitably creepy, bloody one. KISS fans as well will especially appreciate this font task.

This project uses the Crystallize tool in an unusual way. Typically, the Crystallize tools (and their Liquify tool cousins on the Warp tool tearoff) are used to click and drag on paths, creating a crazy but uncontrolled (and more or less random) distortion in shapes. Here, however, you use the crystallization as a much more finely tuned tool for generating tweaks between anchors.

(1) Open a new document. Press T to select the Type tool. Press Command/Ctrl+T to view the Character palette. In the Character palette, select Times New Roman Regular, and set Font Size to 36 pt. Type **DRACULA**.

(2) Select the type with the Selection tool, and press Command/Ctrl+O to convert the type to outline type. Tweak the spacing a bit by hand so that there is a little more space between the *R* and the first *A*.

TIP

An easy way to do this is to use the Group Selection tool to select the letters *ACULA*. Use the right cursor key on your keyboard to make some space between the *R* and the first *A*, while maintaining the spacing for the rest of the letters.

(3) Pretty scary typeface, huh? Relax, I'm kidding. There's more. With the outlined type selected, double-click on the Crystallize tool (part of the Warp tool tearoff), and select these settings:

* **Width:** .03 inches (regardless of unit of measurement settings, just type **.03 in**).

* **Height:** .12 inches

* **Angle:** 0°

* **Intensity:** 100%

* **Complexity:** 0

* **Detail:** 1

* **Brush Affects Anchor Points**

* **Show Brush Size**

(4) Select the letter D, and zoom in very close with the Zoom tool. Starting with the serifs, place the center of the Crystallize tool oval between the control points and click (do *not* click and *drag*—just click). The control points that fall within the tool oval will move vertically up or down, away from the center of the tool to the edge of the tool oval.

(5) In many cases, you will want to emphasize the Crystallize effect by clicking a second time, closer to one specific anchor you want to move further. The trick is to align the center point of the Crystallize tool oval so that there is space inside the oval for the effect to stretch out.

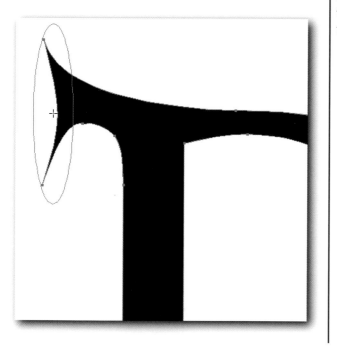

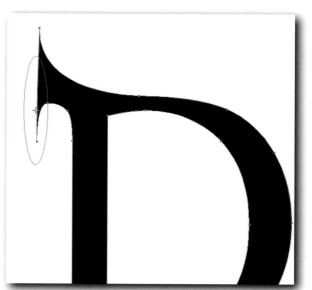

6 Use the Crystallize tool to distort other control points on the top and bottom sides of letter *D*. Use the Add Anchor Point tool (or the Delete Anchor Point tool) as necessary to adjust the number of anchors affected by the Crystallize tool. (I applied no fill to the following figure to make it easier to see the resulting anchors. The final type should be black.)

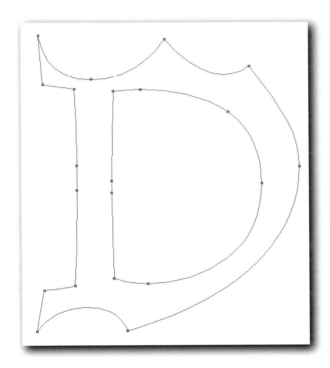

7 Apply the same Crystallize tool settings to anchors on the serif, and the outside curve of the *R*, using the figure as a *general* guide.

8 Once again, this time on the *A*, apply the same Crystallize tool settings to anchors on the serif, and outside curve. Use the figure for inspiration.

9 By now, you've got the hang of using the Crystallize tool on line segments between anchors. Use the Crystallize tool with these settings to create pointed line segments between anchors on the rest of the letters.

10 To complete the type effect, you're going to apply a short, wide Crystallize brush to some of the line segments (such as the tops of the *A*s). To change settings, double-click the Crystallize tool and set reverse width and height settings:

* Set width to .12 inches (type **.12 in**).
* Set height to .03 inches.

11 Apply the new Crystallize brush settings to the control point that you want to move horizontally. In some cases, you might need to add a new anchor (like to the top of the letter *A*) so there is a line segment to which you can apply crystallization.

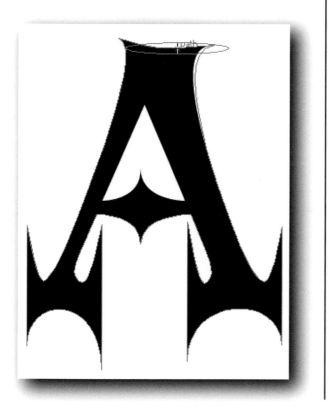

12 Fine-tune some of the crystallized curves by defining a round, .05-inch Crystallize brush to adjust the tops of the *A*s, the *C*, and the *L* serifs.

13 Experiment with gradient fills to finish the job.

Bloody Type

Drops of blood are ubiquitous in illustration — in part because goth is always cool, and in part because of the violent state of the world in which we live.

This task shows you how to create drops that work well with the Vampire-type font you designed in the previous task. But hang onto these steps because they come in handy any time you need to bloody up some type.

1 If you didn't create the type in Task 42, create some type and convert it to outlines (Command/Ctrl+ Shift+O). Fill the type with a linear gradient, and apply a black stroke. Or, if you did create the type in Task 42, use that here.

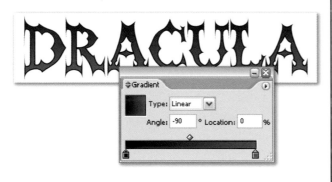

2 Select the type you created in Step 1 (or the type project from Task 42). Align the stroke to the inside (behind the fill) in the Stroke palette.

3 Tweak the anchors in your letters with the Direct Selection tool to fine-tune the look of your characters.

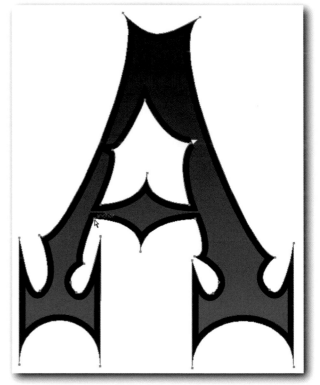

4 Draw a teardrop. Start with an ellipse (drawn with the Ellipse tool) with a black stroke. Adjust the handles of the top anchor control point handles (with the Convert Anchor Point tool) to convert the ellipse into a teardrop.

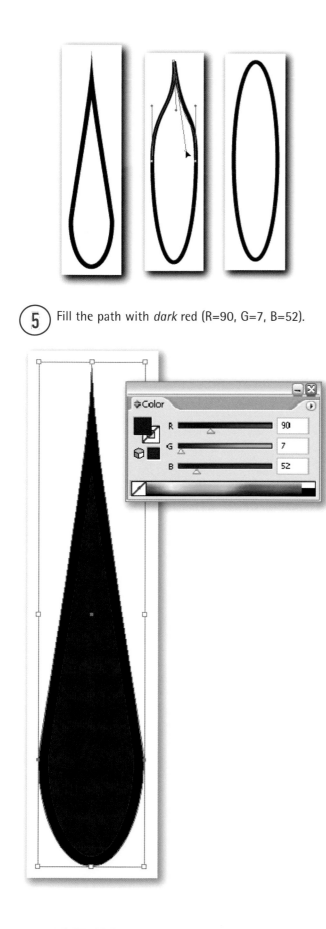

5 Fill the path with *dark* red (R=90, G=7, B=52).

6 Draw a small circle on top of the teardrop. Fill that oval with a lighter red (R=237, G=20, B=90).

7 Generate a smooth blend between the teardrop and the oval. Set Blend options by choosing Object ⇨ Blend ⇨ Blend Options, and select Smooth from the Spacing popup. Use the Blend tool (W) to click on both the inner circle and the outer teardrop to generate the blend. Blending aficionados know that you can fine-tune a blend by selecting which anchor you click in the first and second blend objects. But such finesse isn't really needed here—just click on the path around the circle, and again on the path around the teardrop.

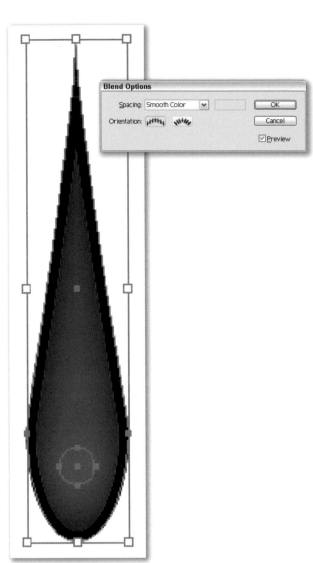

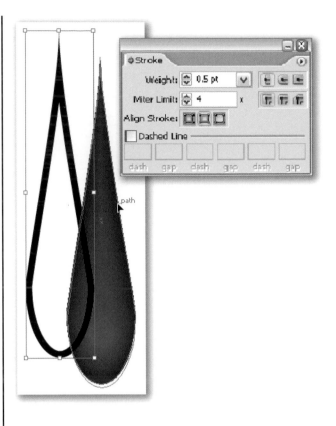

8 Copy the outside shape and paste it on top. Apply no fill to the copy. Apply the same stroke attributes (including Align to Stroke Inside in the Align Stroke area of the Stroke palette). Group all objects.

9 Place copies of the blood drop along the bottom of your letters. Scale each drop using the bottom handle of the bounding box while holding down the Shift key (to maintain proportion when resizing).

10 With the entire project selected, choose Object ⇨ Envelope Distort ⇨ Make With Warp. In the Warp Options dialog box, apply these settings:

* Choose Bulge from the Style popup.
* Select the Horizontal radio button.
* Set bend to 50%.
* Apply no Horizontal or Vertical Distortion.

11 Hang onto those blood droplets — you'll use them some day. In the meantime, you've got some good vampire script.

Effected Type

In Task 38 (see Chapter 8), I use one of Illustrator's graphic styles applied to type. These graphic styles have a number of extremely powerful features, including the ability to apply features such as gradients that normally can't be applied to type. Creating one is very much like creating your own font because graphic styles are savable, and can be used with any Illustrator file.

The other crazy thing about type with graphic styles applied is that it is editable as type. I strongly suggest that you try to finalize on your text *before* you start applying graphic styles because every time you edit the text, the styles have to be re-applied, and that takes time. But, in a pinch, you *can* edit type to which graphic styles have been applied.

In this task, I combine some of the 3D effects that you've been introduced to in other chapters, with graphic styles.

(1) Type the letter **A**. You'll use this letter as a model for your graphic style, and then later you can apply that style to any character. Apply 36-point Myriad (Adobe's "house font").

(2) Apply a Warp effect to the selected type by choosing Effect ⇨ Warp ⇨ Arc. In the Warp Options dialog box, choose Arc from the Style popup and set Bend to 0%. In the Direction area, set Horizontal to 50%, and Vertical to –50%.

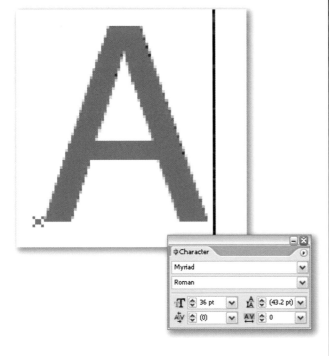

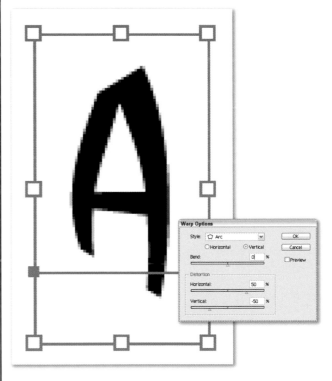

CAUTION

Do not convert this type to outlines. Much of the fun lies in the fact that this task uses completely editable type.

3 Apply an Extrude effect by choosing Effect ⇨ 3D ⇨ Extrude & Bevel. In the 3D Extrude & Bevel Options dialog box, set X-Axis rotation to –8 degrees, Y-Axis rotation to –10 degrees, and Z-Axis rotation to 6 degrees. Set Perspective to 0, and Extrude Depth to 38 points. Set Shading Color to Yellow.

4 With both the Warp and Extrude effects applied to the type (and remember: It's still *type* – editable type), take a look at the Appearance palette. Both effects are displayed. Drag this set of effects into the Graphic Styles palette. Call the graphic style **Jar Wars**. Alternately, you can select the letter, and choose Add to Graphic Styles from the Graphic Styles palette.

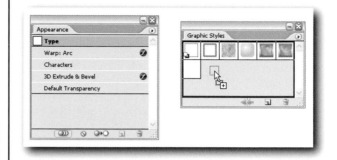

5 Type a bit of normal text into a text box; draw the box first with the Type tool, and enter three short lines of text. Click the Jar Wars graphic style in the Graphic Styles palette to apply that set of effects to the type.

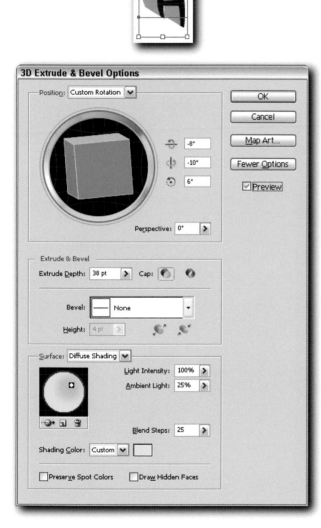

6 The type is editable. You can change the type size, font, or color. Or even spell-check it! The graphic style is available for other type, or other projects. Touch up the illustration by tweaking the type box rotation and adding a background. You might have the background from Task 10, shown here.

3D Flushed Type

Normal illustration books might provide an example of right-, left-, or full-justified flush type. Not so here. This is *flushed* type. I can't remember if toilets flush clockwise in the Southern Hemisphere, or in the Northern Hemisphere. But somewhere in the world I got this right.

Some of the tasks here "are inspired by" the very first project in the book (Task 1 in Chapter 1). Here, however, the perspective is radically changed, and I introduce some new tricks to create the flushed type look.

1 Create a new file, and draw a circle with a diameter of 6 inches. Apply a color fill and no stroke. (It is important to assign no stroke color.) Applying no stroke reduces the number of useless mapping surfaces you need to sort through when you map type on an extrusion of this circle. The fill color won't affect the final project; it's just to help you find the circle.

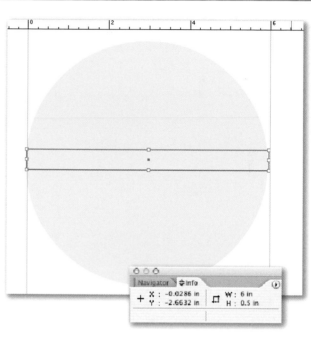

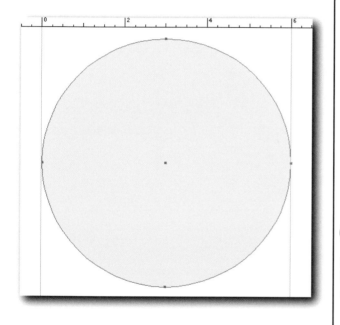

2 Draw a rectangle, ½ inch high, and the diameter of the circle. Apply no fill or stroke — this rectangle is just for sizing purposes.

3 Drag the rectangle off the circle. Type a line of text. Convert the type to outlines, and resize it to fill the rectangle, leaving just a small amount of space above, below, and on the sides between the enlarged text and the rectangle.

ROUND AND ROUND AND ROUND WE GO... WHERE WE STOP - NOBODY KNOWS

④ Use the Align palette to center the text horizontally and vertically in the rectangle. Group the text and rectangle. Duplicate vertically to create 16 copies of the type. Then, drag all the type rectangles into the Symbols palette to create a mappable symbol.

⑤ Select the circle, and choose Effect ➪ 3D ➪ Extrude & Bevel. If your system can handle it, click the Preview checkbox. If not, fly blind (with my instructions) and you should still be okay.

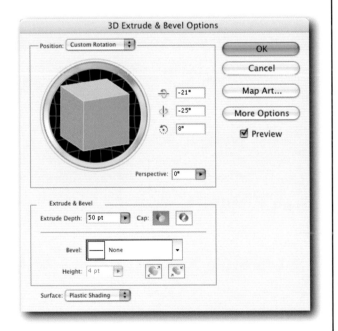

⑥ In the 3D Extrude & Bevel Options dialog box, apply these settings:

* **X-Axis rotation:** –3 degrees
* **Y-Axis rotation:** –6 degrees
* **Z-Axis rotation:** –5 degrees.
* **Perspective:** 160 degrees
* **Extrude Depth:** 1500 pt
* **Bevel:** Rounded
* **Bevel Height:** 4 pt
* **Surface:** Wireframe

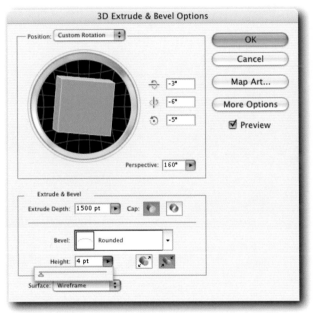

⑦ Click the Map Art button in the 3D Extrude & Bevel dialog box, and locate the mappable surface by relying on the Preview button if you can. Click the Scale to Fit button to size the mappable type to fill the surface. Because the surface is inverted, drag up on the bottom sizing handle until the type is flipped upside down, and then re-align it on the mappable surface. Rotate the type about 45 degrees counterclockwise.

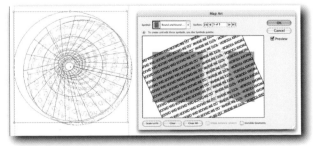

chapter 9 ● cosmic typefaces

8 Strip the wireframe objects from the resulting effect by expanding and ungrouping (about a million times) until you can select and delete the wireframe.

9 Assign a white fill and no stroke to the text. Finish up the project by placing a circle with a spiral gradient fill behind the text.

live paint on parole

Throughout this book, I've integrated Illustrator CS2's two new big things, Live Trace and Live Paint, into tasks. I think it's worth having a (short) chapter that just fixates on Live Paint. On a superficial level, Live Paint allows you to apply color to areas formed at the intersection of any paths. But Live Paint also changes the logic of how Illustrator paths are defined.

Paths in Illustrator have always been selectable, editable, discrete objects, whether they intersect other paths or not. Live Paint allows you to change the rules – not just in how color is applied to strokes and fills, but in how paths are edited. Essentially, Live Paint converts intersected paths into separate paths that are not only paintable but also editable. The projects in this chapter illustrate the implications of this, both for scanned artwork and for drawn projects with a lot of intersecting lines.

Mandala

Mandalas are patterns — often, I hear, with satanic overtones that can be interpreted only by tele-vangelists (similar to what you hear when you play an old Beatles record backwards).

Okay, hidden inner meanings aside, one type of mandala involves circular patterns that are divided into four separate projections of the same, typically rather complex, design. You create one of those here, and then take advantage of Live Paint to break up the myriad of intersecting paths into separate, paintable strokes and fills.

NOTE

For a more useful and rational exploration of the cultural significance of mandalas, including ones that do not involve quartered panels, visit www.mcuniverse.com/Mandalas.915.0.html.

For an interesting discussion of the relationship between mandalas and nature, check out www.lyon-art.com/5-mandalas/1a-mandalas-4.html.

(1) Create a new, letter-sized Illustrator document. Set Stroke to 1 point, black, and set Fill to None.

(2) Draw one horizontal guide 5½ inches from the top, and one vertical guide 4¼ inches from the left (the guides intersect at the center of the artboard).

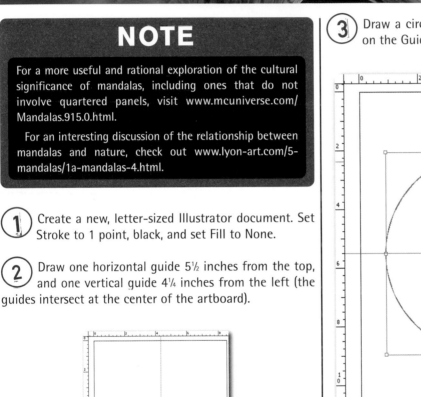

(3) Draw a circle with a diameter of 7 inches centered on the Guide intersection.

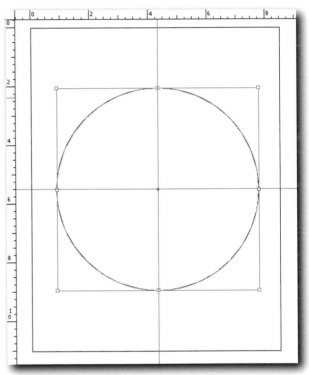

TIP

Draw the circle by clicking on the intersection point of the Guides with the Ellipse tool. Hold down the Option/Alt and Shift key while you drag out from the center. Use Guides or Rulers to determine the size of the circle — sizing does not have to be exact!

4 Use the Pen tool to draw a path as shown on the top half of the circle. You might find a horizontal Guide at about the 4 inch (vertical) mark, which is helpful.

5 Use the Pen tool to draw a curved line on the bottom half of the circle, as shown.

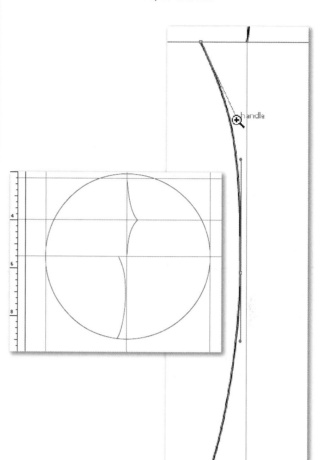

6 Select both curves and group them (Command/ Ctrl+G). Double-click on the Reflect tool (in the Rotate tool tearoff). Click the Horizontal axis radio button, and click Copy to horizontally reflect and copy the two paths along the vertical Guide.

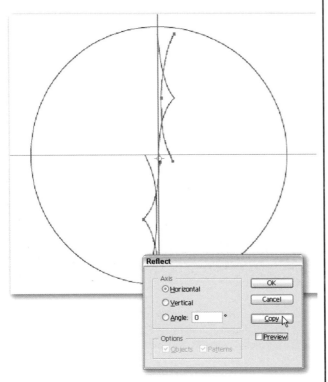

7 Click the Rotate tool once, and click on the intersection of the vertical and horizontal Guides to define the rotation pivot point. Hold down the Shift key to constrain angles to 45 degrees, and hold down the Command/Alt key to duplicate. Click and drag on the end of the selected paths to create a copy rotated 45 degrees.

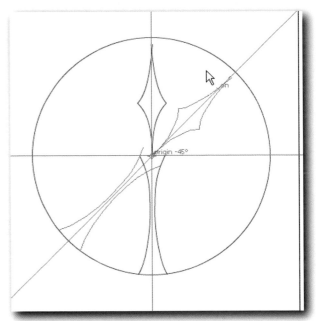

8 Press Command/Ctrl+D (repeat) seven times to complete the design.

9 Convert the whole illustration to a Live Paint region by selecting all the paths, and pressing Option/Alt+Command/Ctrl+X.

10 Double-click on the Live Paint tool in the Toolbox. In the Live Paint Bucket Options dialog box, select the Paint Fills checkbox. Deselect the Paint Strokes checkbox — you will leave the strokes at a discrete 1-point black. Reset the Width to a more sane 8 points.

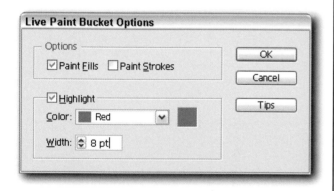

11 Create five Aztec-inspired color swatches:

* R=0, G=167, B=109 (Aztec Green)
* R=236, G=0, B=140 (Aztec Magenta)
* R=94, G=45, B=145 (Aztec Purple)
* R=237, G=28, B=36 (Aztec Red)
* R=255, G=203, B=50 (Aztec Yellow)

12 Select one of the colors in the set of swatches, and use the Live Paint Bucket tool to apply that color to one set of shapes in the design.

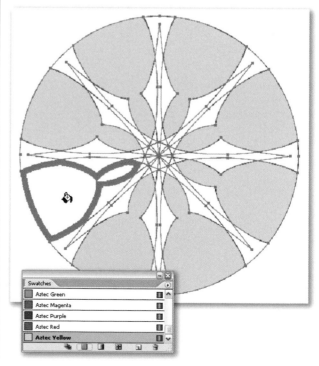

13 Select a second color from the set of swatches and apply it to other fill paths that were generated by the Live Paint tool.

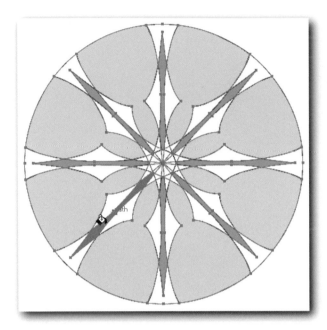

14 Finish by assigning additional colors to the remaining sets of shapes. You'll want to zoom in to Live Paint the small paths in the center of the mandala.

15 Draw a diamond on top of the design as shown.

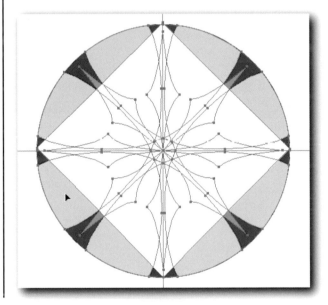

16 As a final touch, use the diamond as a clipping mask. To apply the diamond as a clipping mask, select the diamond and the design (everything) and press Command/Ctrl+7.

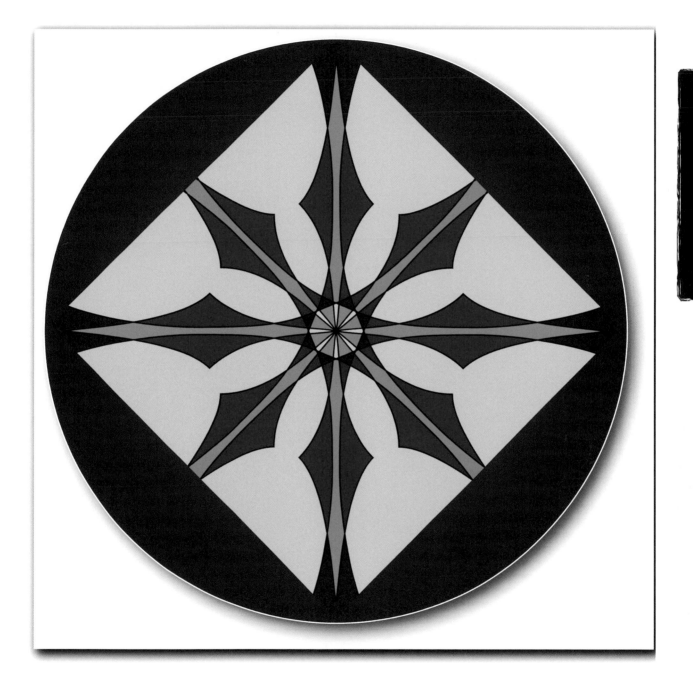

Tracing Roy and Troy

In Task 11, I demonstrate some of the ways you can easily convert comics to Illustrator files by applying fills to scanned comic art. Here, you explore more fully the process of vectorizing pen and ink drawings.

You can download and work with Bruce K. Hopkins' "Roy and Troy" drawing at the book web site (www.illustratorgonewild.com).

① Create a new file in Illustrator, and place the TIFF file "Roy and Troy" on the artboard. Do not link or place the file as a template layer.

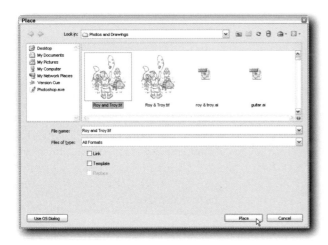

② Click the Live Trace button in the Control palette to access Live Trace settings. Choose Inked Drawing from the Presets popup. Click the Live Paint button to expand the vector paths, and to generate Live Paint regions.

> ### TIP
>
> You can download an Illustrator tracing of "Roy and Troy" at www.illustratorgonewild.com, and apply Live Paint.

③ This project involves applying coloring not only to fills but to strokes as well, so start by defining the Live Paint Bucket to work on fills and strokes. To do that, double-click the Live Paint tool in the Toolbox. In the Live Paint Bucket Options dialog box, select both the Paint Strokes checkbox and the Paint Fills checkbox. Change the Highlight width to 4 points to make selecting strokes more manageable.

④ Use the Live Paint Bucket to select Live Paint regions, and apply the selected fill to that region.

5 Areas that were not defined as Live Paint regions because the gaps in paths were too large cannot be individually painted. With the Live Paint region selected, click the Gap Options button in the Control palette to open the Gap Options dialog box. Set the Gap Detection to Small Gaps, and try again to paint troublesome regions. After you narrow the gap settings, complete the process of applying fills to newly generated Live Paint regions.

TIP

If there are regions with really small gaps that you want to dam up, experiment with smaller gap settings in the Custom area of the Gap Options dialog box.

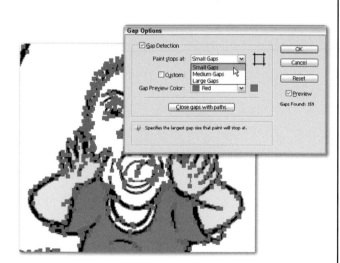

6 Live Paint regions allow you to apply color to strokes, as well as fills. As you hover over a stroke, the Live Paint Bucket icon changes into a brush. Apply coloring to strokes. You can adjust the width of the applied stroke as well as the color in the Control palette.

Live Paint Survival Skills

You will probably want to *edit* paths in normal Illustrator mode. When you weary of applying color to Live Paint regions, choose Object ⇨ Live Paint ⇨ Expand to convert strokes and fills to normal Illustrator properties. Later, when you want to toggle back into Live Paint mode, you can select just some paths, and convert them back to Live Paint regions (with the paths selected, press Option/Alt+Command/Ctrl+X).

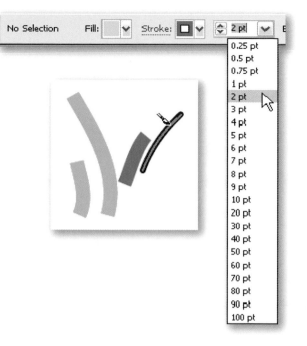

7 In Live Paint mode, you encounter a different logic for defining a stroke. In Live Paint regions, *every* line segment formed by the intersection of lines is a distinct path. You can apply different stroke attributes to sections of a path that have been intersected by other lines.

8 To apply a uniform color to an area with small gaps (in other words, if you want the fill to ignore even small gaps, and just keep spreading), re-access the Gap Options dialog box by clicking the Gap icon in the Control palette. Select Large Gaps in the Gap Detection area.

Large Gaps, Small Gaps?

When filling sections of a Live Paint region with color, it is quicker to apply color to regions with the Gap Detection option in the Gap Options dialog box set to Large Gaps. The Large Gaps option means that the *relatively* large gaps between (almost) touching paths will "close up" for the purposes of applying a fill color. Setting Gap Detection to Small Gaps provides more control over where paint flows, so choose the Small Gap option if you want Live Paint to apply only in areas where the gaps between paths are very small.

The Preview checkbox displays the gaps on the artboard. If necessary, define your own custom gap width, noting the effect on the artboard. The Gaps Found value in the Gap Options dialog box gives you a sense of how many regions different settings will create.

(9) Continue to apply Live Paint fills and stroke coloring to complete the illustration.

Win a CD Cover Design Contest

This project is about me trying to win a free CD. I simply need to design a CD cover for a radio station that features their call letters (as in KXYZ). The station's web site promises that they're going to throw in a copy of Illustrator CS2 if I win!

What's in this for you? This task involves placing outlined letters on top of each other. Then, I use Live Paint to apply some dissonant coloring to sections of the letters formed by where the letters intersect. Do a Google search on this; I bet somewhere, someone is looking for someone to design a CD cover for free.

1 Type the call letters of a radio station in your area that is offering prizes for a new logo. Short of that, just type the call letters of your favorite radio station in Impact font. Font size doesn't matter here.

2 Press Command/Ctrl+Shift+O to convert the type to outlined letters.

3 Select the grouped outlined text, and resize so the letters are large enough to manipulate. Select Object ➪ Ungroup to break each letter into its own object.

4 Resize and rearrange the letters so there is significant overlap between them.

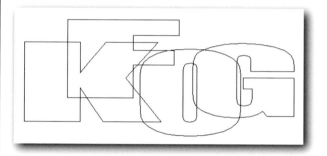

5 For this project you will be applying Live Paint Bucket colors to both strokes and fills. Double-click the Live Paint tool and click both the Paint Fills and Paint Strokes checkboxes.

6 Select all the letters, and press Option/Alt+ Command/Ctrl+X to convert all the letters into a Live Paint region. Each intersected area becomes a uniquely paintable area. Choose a set of color swatches, and use the Live Paint Bucket tool to apply colors to letters. Disrupt but don't destroy the viewer's cognitive process by applying different colors to overlapped areas.

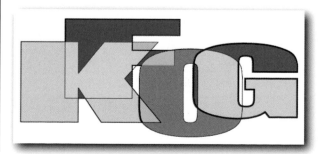

7 Next, focus on strokes. Selectively apply white to stroke segments with the Live Paint tool.

8 To prepare to place your letters on top of a background, use the Live Paint Bucket to apply no fill to selected areas.

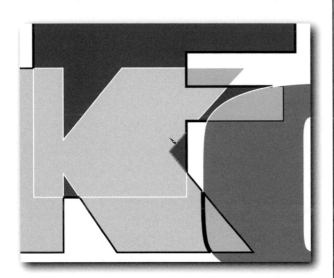

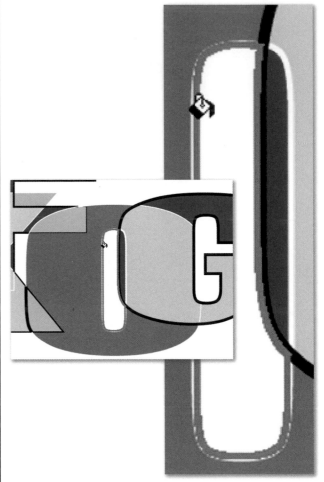

9 Touch up the project by placing a background behind the station call letters.

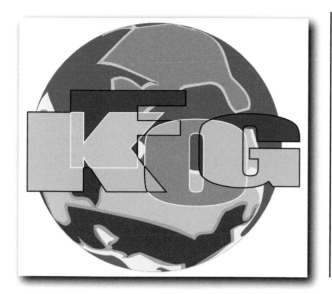

10 If the contest rules require your illustration to fit on a CD cover (or, if you just happen to be designing a CD cover), draw a 5.469-inch square over the illustration, select both the square and the design, and select Object ➪ Crop Area ➪ Make to apply the square as a crop area for the CD cover to complete the project.

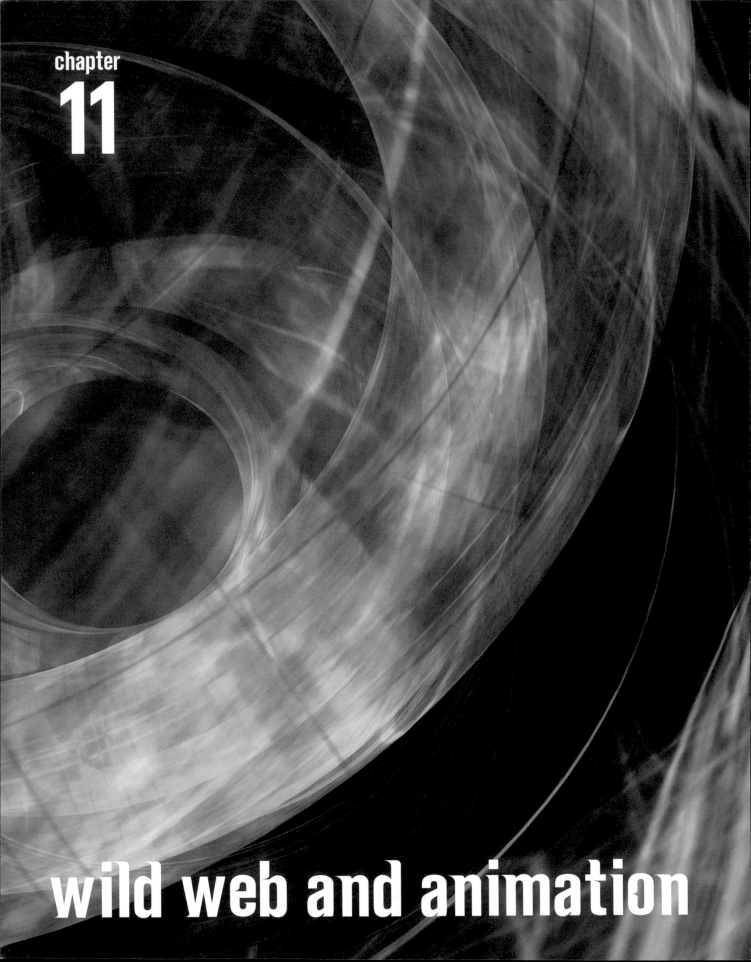

wild web and animation

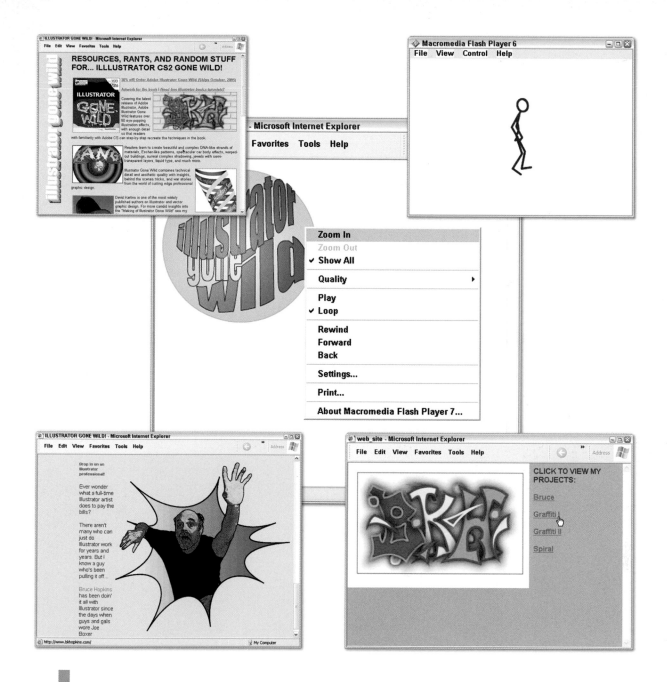

In this final chapter, you learn to create exportable graphics and animation for display on the web. If you haven't played with Macromedia Flash before, you may be surprised by how much Flash you can squeeze out of Illustrator's export to Flash tools.

Illustrator's ability to export to Flash frames is useful both to preserve vector scalability and to create animations that someone will work with in Flash. Illustrator's Save for Web feature includes primitive but functional tools for creating a Flash animation. In this chapter, I show you how to use the two basic types of layers-to-frames techniques for generating Flash animation from Illustrator. In short, the "build" frames option is better for *morphing* (animated transition between shapes) animation, and the "sequence" method is better for *tweening* (generating transitional frames between defined "key" frames).

Building an Animated Banner

There are, as I noted in this chapter's introduction, two basic ways to generate animation from Illustrator. The first, which you do in this task, involves "building" up animation frames by piling on pieces of an animation. The second, which I show you in the next task, involves *sequencing*, which is like rotating different frames — essentially displaying one path at a time.

Built animations are more spectacular, and are more attuned to morphing and *tweening*-like animation effects. In general, you need a *lot* of layers for a built animation. But that doesn't mean you have to *create* a lot of layers. Illustrator handles that.

---

1 Design a logo with type.

2 From the Layers palette fly-out menu, choose Release to Layers (Build). A layer is generated from every object. Feel free to examine the logic of how layers are built up from the back to the front of your illustration.

NOTE

When you release to layers, the generated layers are sub-layers. Normally, this doesn't have much impact on the eventual Flash animation. Sometimes, sublayers create odd little blips in the timing of an animation. I address that issue later in the sidebar "Sublayers, Layers, and Odd Timing" in this chapter.

Do's and Don'ts of Exporting to Flash

Normally, *don't* worry too much about how you prepare the illustration for conversion to Flash frames because Illustrator, intuitively, builds up from your bottom-most object. *Don't* be too conservative about using blends, gradients, and meshes. Your visitors' systems have 16-bit color or more, and they can see millions, not hundreds, of colors. This is a book about *wild* illustration, so you and I don't give a $%@# about how the animation will appear on a black-and-white cell phone.

Don't worry too much about size — your Flash movie can be rescaled in a web design program such as Dreamweaver. On the other hand, you might as well create a banner or logo about the size in which it will display, just so you can see how it is going to look. *Do* outline type. If you want each character to be a separate object (and end up in a separate Flash frame) ungroup all the character groups that are generated when you convert type to outlines. *Do* be aggressive in expanding appearances of effects — file size does matter. Long Flash "movies" (as SWF files are referred to) are a big online "go away" sign.

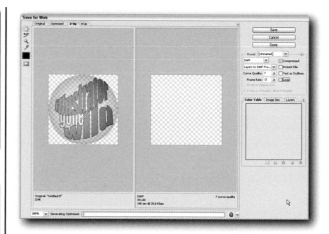

NOTE

Frame rate depends on the processing speed of a viewer's computer, and download time. Download time is obviously linked to file size; therefore the options I'm having you select are designed to hack that down to something a visitor can tolerate. Between download time (which defines when the Flash animation starts) and computer processing speed, frame rates should be considered a relative value. Twelve frames per second creates the smooth animation effect you want here.

6 Click Save to export the layers to Flash frames. In the Save Optimized As dialog box, navigate to the folder with your web site media files, and enter a filename. Click Save again to save the file as an SWF in your web site folder.

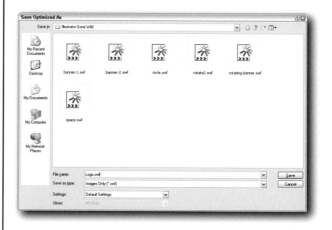

3 Select File ⇨ Save for Web to open the Save for Web window.

4 From the Optimized File Format popup menu, choose SWF.

5 In the Type of Export popup, choose Layers to SWF Frames. Set Curve Quality to 7. (Higher values create more accurate curves, and slightly increase file size and download time. Lower values don't reduce download time that much, so it's not worth it to make curve quality much lower than 7.) For a smoothly animated logo, set the Frame Rate to 12 (frames per second). Select the Loop checkbox to repeat the animation indefinitely (or not, if you want your animation to play once and then stop, displaying the final logo). Select the Compressed checkbox to further reduce file size.

7 The Flash movie is ready to place in a web page. You can use the following code to embed the file with a white background. Change the "movie" and "file" parameters to the path to your SWF file. Change the width and height values to reflect the size of your Flash movie.

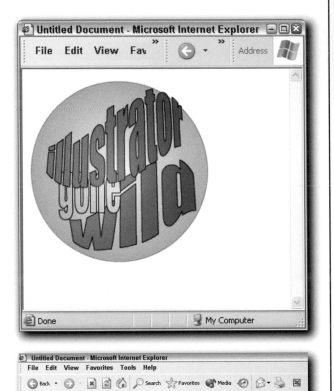

TIP

If you're using Dreamweaver, choose Insert ⇨ Media ⇨ Flash and use the Dreamweaver Properties Inspector to define the movie parameters. If you just want to preview your SWF movie, open it in your web browser. Assuming your browser has the Flash Player plug-in, you can test the movie in your browser.

```
<object classid="clsid:D27CDB6E-AE6D-11cf-
96B8-444553540000" codebase="http://down-
load.macromedia.com/pub/shockwave/cabs/flash
/swflash.cab#version=6,0,29,0" width="240"
height="240" title="Logo">
   <param name="movie" value="file:///C⇨/
Logo.swf">
   <param name="quality" value="high">
   <embed src="file: Logo.swf" quality="high"
pluginspage="http://www.macromedia.com/go/
getflashplayer" type="application/x-shock-
wave-flash" width="239" height="240"></embed>
</object>.
```

NOTE

Watch my animated logo at www.illustratorgonewild.com.

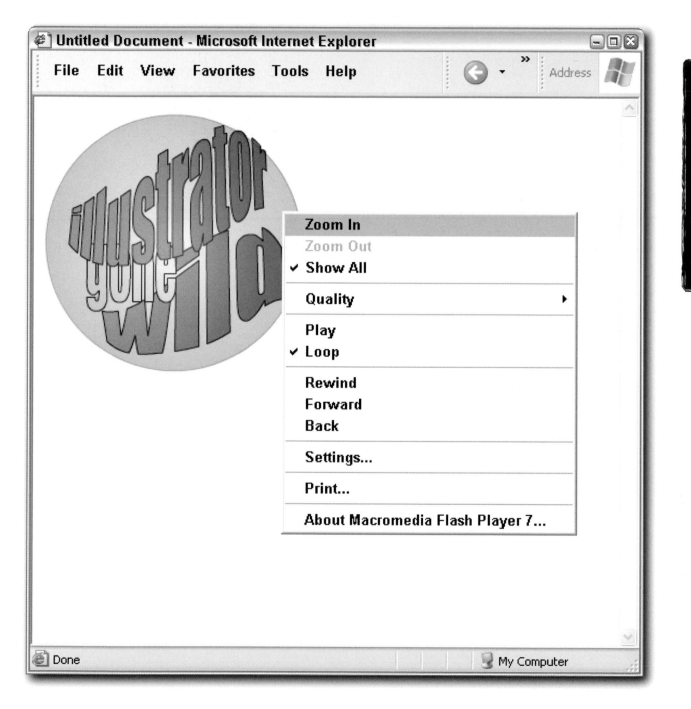

Sequencing an Animated Banner

The previous Illustrator-to-Flash projects have used the Build method for automatically generating layers. With that method, each layer becomes a frame, and the resulting animation *adds* frames, so that the final image displays *all* the frames in the original illustration.

In this project, I show you how to use *sequencing* to generate animation. With sequenced layers, the resulting animation displays one frame after another, but does not accumulate frames.

I'm going to make a Flash banner for the web site for this book. You can see it (or something like it) live at www.illustratorgonewild.com. If you create a banner for the book's site, send it to me. If I use it at the site, I'll be happy to credit you and make you (in)famous.

If you're doing your own thing, substitute different text in the following steps:

1 Create a new file using the 800 × 600 Artboard Setup preset.

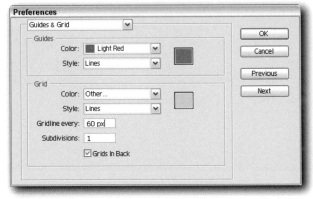

2 Set units of measurement to pixels (choose Illustrator/Edit ⇨ Preferences ⇨ Units & Display, and select Pixels from the General popup). In the Guides & Grid panel of the Preferences dialog box, define Gridline every 60 pixels, with just 1 Subdivision. After you OK the preferences, choose View ⇨ Show Grid.

③ Create your web site banner type. Use Impact font when you create type to which you will apply graphic styles. Impact is the most useful and flexible font. Resize the type to fit in the 720 × 60 pixel area defined by your grids. Convert to outlines (Shift+Command/Ctrl+O) to reduce file size.

④ Copy the type. Choose Window ➪ Graphic Style Libraries ➪ Text Effects, and choose one of the graphic styles to apply to your selected, outlined type.

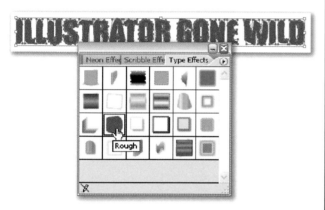

⑤ Copy the type again, and apply a second graphic style to the copied type.

⑥ Create a few more copies of the type, and apply other graphic styles to the copies.

NOTE

If you want to create your own graphic styles, refer back to Task 38 and Task 44 for projects that demonstrate how that is done.

CAUTION

Avoid graphic styles (or any effects) that distort the *size* or *shape* of the type very much. Adding a bit of size from drop shadows and so on is okay, but wild distortion, enveloping, warping, and tilting will increase the size of the Flash window.

Sublayers, Layers, and Odd Timing

Oddly enough, Illustrator generates sublayers within an initial layer (Layer 1 by default). In most cases, this isn't a big issue. However, the "extra" layer does cause a glitch in the timing of the Flash movie. If you are exporting to Flash format, and will not be touching up your animation in Flash, and if this timing glitch bothers you, convert the sublayers to layers by Shift-clicking on all of them and dragging them into the Layers palette above Layer 1 — thus converting them from sublayers to layers. This trick fixes the little timing glitch in how your animation displays in the Flash player or online in a web site.

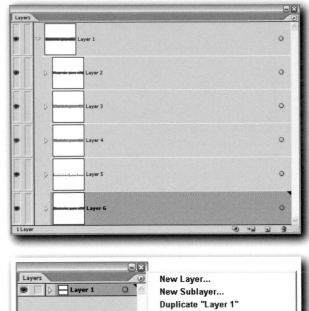

(7) Delete the original type (with no graphic styles or effects). Select all the remaining text and expand the appearance of all the effects to reduce the final file size (choose Object ➪ Expand Appearance).

(8) Use the Align palette, and align all the copies of your type both vertically centered and horizontally centered (so they are on top of each other).

(9) From the Layers palette fly-out menu, choose Release to Layers (Sequence). The Release to Layers Build option is useful for some types of animation, where you want to "stack" objects on top of each other to create smoother animation. Here, you're creating a rotating banner, not a "tweened" animation, so the Release to Layers (Sequence) feature is more appropriate.

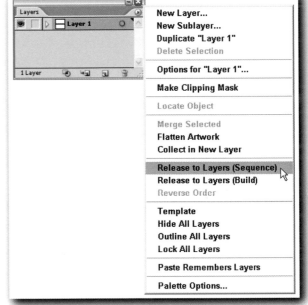

(10) Draw a rectangle over the 720 pixel by 60 pixel area that constrains your different layers. Choose Object ➪ Crop Area ➪ Make (or press Command/Ctrl+7) to constrain the generated Flash file to this area.

(11) Check to make sure there are no stray elements you don't want converted to SWF frames. Clean up any stray junk.

(12) Choose File ⇨ Save for Web. Click the Optimized tab (in the upper-left corner of the Save for Web window). From the Optimized File Format popup menu, choose SWF. In the Type of Export popup, choose Layers to SWF Frame. Set Curve Quality to 7. (Higher values create more accurate curves, and slightly increase file size and download time. Lower values don't reduce download time that much, so it's not worth it to make curve quality much lower than 7.) For an animated banner that changes, but doesn't strobe, set the Frame Rate very low — like .2 (frames per second). Select the Loop checkbox to repeat the animation indefinitely. Select the Compressed checkbox to further reduce file size. Click Save to export the layers to Flash frames. Click Save to open the Save Optimized As dialog box.

NOTE

A rate of two-tenths of a frame per second displays each of your rotating banners for *about* five seconds.

(13) In the Save Optimized As dialog box, enter a filename and navigate to the folder with your web site's Flash, media, or image files. After the file is exported to Flash, it can be placed in a web site, where it will play.

Got Code?

If you need some HTML to add this banner to a page (using, in this case, the SWF filename banner-1), feel free to copy and paste this. The code here displays the SWF animation at high quality, 720 pixels wide and 60 pixels high (feel free to adjust those values), with no spacing around it. If you want spacing, change the hspace (horizontal spacing) or vspace (vertical spacing) values from zero.

Autoplay and looping are defaults and no special attributes are required for that. This code also sends viewers without a Flash player to a page where they can download the player. Use your own hexadecimal color value for the background color (replace my # FFFFFF (white) with your own background color for a transparent-looking background):

```
<object classid="clsid:D27CDB6E-AE6D-11cf-
96B8-444553500000" codebase="http://down-
load.macromedia.com/pub/shockwave/cabs/flash
/swflash.cab#version=6,0,29,0" width="720"
height="60" hspace="0" vspace="0"
title="Flash banner">
        <param name="movie" value="banner-
1.swf">
        <param name="quality" value="high">
<param name="BGCOLOR" value="#D5DADE">
        <embed src="banner-1.swf" width=
"720" height="60" hspace="0" vspace="0"
quality="high" pluginspage="http://www.
macromedia.com/go/getflashplayer" type=
"application/x-shockwave-flash" bgcolor=
"#FFFFFF"></embed>
        </object>
```

14 Want to break the mold on banners? Rotate the banner 90 degrees counterclockwise (constrain rotation with the Shift key), and have it display vertically on the left side of your web page. Do the rotation in Illustrator before you generate the Flash movie. And you're done!

Animation from the Blender

A quick and effective — and fun — way to create animated cartoons in Illustrator is to generate "tweened" images from step blends, and then expand the blends. Each of the generated objects can be sequenced to a layer, and then saved as animation frames in an SWF file.

As you did in the last project, you use sequencing to build layers for animation here. That way, your walking stick figures appear to be in motion — as opposed to simply building up an illustration. This is about as close as any (semi)rational person will want to get to actually creating animated Flash cartoons directly from Illustrator.

NOTE

This project requires elements created in Task 23.

1 Create at least one step blend between stick men. Three is even better. If you use more than one blend, line up the blends so they are more or less vertically aligned, and more or less evenly spaced.

2 After you generate the step blend, choose Object ⇨ Blend ⇨ Expand to convert the generated blend paths to objects.

3 Select all of the (now) grouped sets of stick men, and ungroup them so the stick men are not grouped with other stick men. Don't ungroup so far that you break up the individual stick men into ungrouped objects. From the Layers palette fly-out menu, choose Release to Layers (Sequence).

CAUTION

Before you generate the layers, check the stacking order of your paths. The bottom (back) paths become the first frames, and the top paths become the later layers. Then, after you generate layers, you can review the order of the layers. If you find some layers out of order, you can re-order them by clicking and dragging up or down in the Layers palette.

4 Choose File ⇨ Save for Web. Click the 2-up tab (in the upper-left corner of the Save for Web window). The 2-up window allows you to see the original image for reference. Select the bottom preview window. From the Optimized File Format popup menu, choose SWF. In the Type of Export popup, choose Layers to SWF Frame. Set Curve Quality to 7. (Higher values create more accurate curves, and slightly increase file size and download time.) Set the Frame Rate to a standard 12 frames per second. Select the Loop checkbox to repeat the animation indefinitely. Select the Compressed checkbox to further reduce file size. Click Save to export the layers to Flash frames.

5 Preview the animation by choosing a browser from the Select Browser window. Click Save to open the Save Optimized As dialog box.

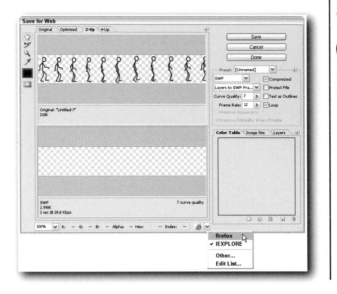

6 Jump back into Illustrator's Save for Web window. In the Save Optimized As dialog box, enter a filename and navigate to the folder with your web site's Flash, media, or image files. After the file is exported to Flash, it can be placed in a web site, where it will play.

7 You can preview your animation either in the Flash player (downloadable from www.flashplayer.com) or by opening the file in a browser window (provided your browser has the Flash Player plug-in).

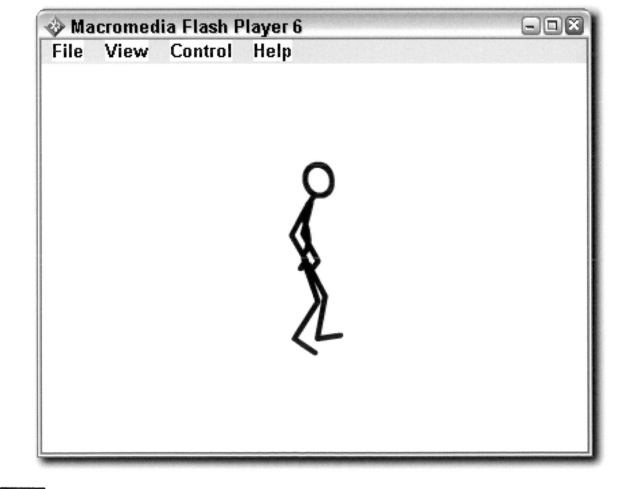

Transparent Web Pix

In this quick task, I show you how to take the image of illustrator Bruce K. Hopkins jumping out of a puckered shape that you (might have) created in Task 19, and turn it into a high-quality transparent online image.

One challenge you face with illustrations like this is that the GIF format can't handle the number of colors and the color gradation in this illustration. I claimed earlier that the gradients, blends, and meshes you use in Illustrator work online. But I lied. Not really, but there's a qualifier involved — they work well with JPEG format images. To get around this conundrum, I use the PNG ("ping") format, which supports both transparency and gradients.

① Open the file breakout.ai or whatever you called the file you created in Task 19.

> ## NOTE
>
> Instead of using breakout.ai, you can do the rest of this task with a simple shape. Create an ellipse and apply some pucker (Effect ⇨ Distort & Transform ⇨ Pucker & Bloat, and apply some pucker. Then, apply a gradient fill.

Choose File ➭ Save for Web. In the Save for Web window, click the Optimized tab (at the top of the window). From the Optimized Format popup, choose PNG-24. Click the Transparency checkbox. Also, click the Interlaced checkbox.

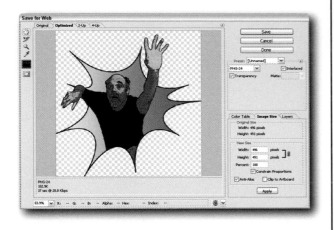

You can see download time in the lower-left corner of the Save for Web window. To change the connection speed at which download time is calculated, Ctrl/right-click on the download time and choose a connection speed.

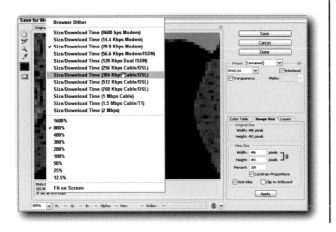

TIP

Interlacing makes waiting for an image to download more tolerable by "fading in" an image instead of having it appear on a page in stripes as it downloads. If you want to resize the image for the web, click the Image Size tab and adjust sizing there.

To preview your image in a web browser, choose a browser from the Select Browser menu popup. The image opens in a blank web page.

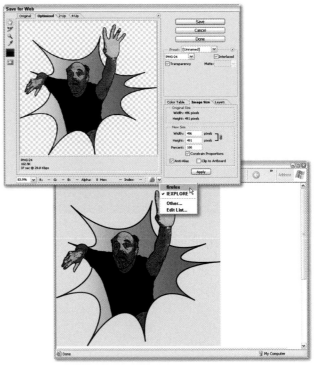

5 After previewing the image in a browser, jump back to Illustrator's Save for Web window and click the Save button. In the Save Optimized dialog box, navigate to the folder with your web site images, and enter a filename. Click Save. Your image is ready to embed in a web page.

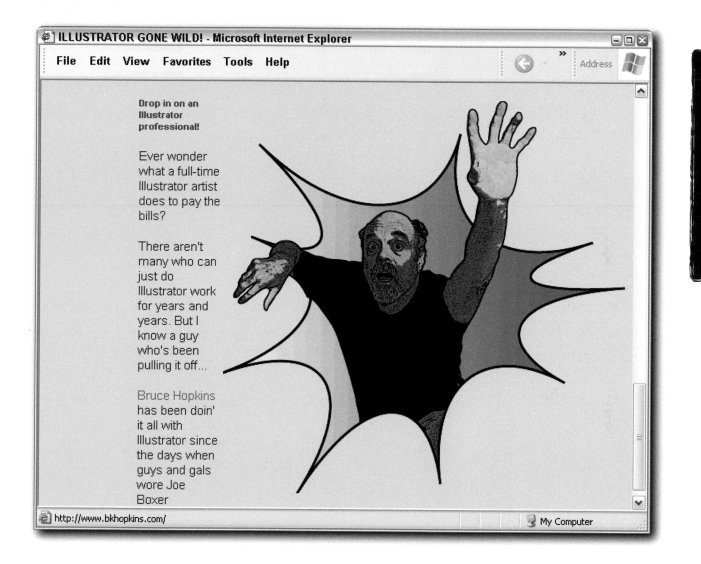

Creating a Fab Favicon

This project is as "gone wild" as a 16-pixel illustration can get. Another way to look at it is that this is the *tiniest* project in this book! *Favicons* — those wonderful little icons that make your web site stand out in your visitor's title bar and bookmarks list are restricted to 16 pixels square.

It might seem counterintuitive to design these rasterized babies in a high-powered vector design program such as Illustrator. If you calculate the cost of creating one of these things, how much is it per pixel? Oddly enough, Illustrator is by far my favorite way to design a cool favicon. Go ahead and vectorize an interesting (if tiny) icon, and let Illustrator worry about how to convert it to a 16-pixel-square thingy.

(1) Start by creating a new file, 16 × 16 pixels.

New Document

Name: favicon	OK
	Cancel

Artboard Setup

Size: Custom   Width: 16 px

Units: Pixels   Height: 16 px

Orientation:

Color Mode

○ CMYK Color   ● RGB Color

(2) Zoom like crazy — to something like 800%. More and you'll have a hard time envisioning the way your favicon will look. Design an icon.

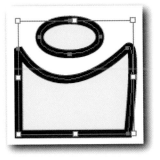

(3) Choose File ➪ Export, and select the BMP bitmap format. Type **favicon** in the File name field. Illustrator assigns a .bmp filename extension. Don't fight it — just rename the file later. Click Export. The Rasterize Options dialog box appears.

Export

Save in:	Illustrator Gone Wild

Desktop
My Documents
My Pictures
My Computer
My Network Place:
Version Cue
Photoshop.exe

File name:	favicon.bmp
Format:	BMP (*.BMP)
Version Comments:	BMP (*.BMP)
	Enhanced Metafile (*.EMF)
	JPEG (*.JPG)
	Macintosh PICT (*.PCT)
	Macromedia Flash (*.SWF)
	Photoshop (*.PSD)
	PNG (*.PNG)
	Targa (*.TGA)
	Text Format (*.TXT)
	TIFF (*.TIF)

Use OS Dialog

4 In the Rasterize Options dialog box, choose the Screen option in the Resolution popup. Check the Anti-Alias checkbox to reduce jaggies, and then click OK.

5 In the BMP Options dialog box, choose 16 Bit color. This is the highest color set supported by browsers for favicons. Click OK.

6 Rename favicon.bmp as **favicon.ico** in your operating system file manager, or in your Web design software. FTP the file into the root folder of your web site.

CAUTION

Browser support for favicons is still not fully standardized. Mozilla and Safari provide more reliable favicon display than Internet Explorer. Some browsers are more likely to detect a favicon if you place the following code in the Head section of your web page HTML:

```
<link rel="SHORTCUT ICON" href="/
favicon.ico">
```

7 Call all your friends. Now. Tell them to bookmark your site and enjoy your favicon.

Bookmarks **Tools** **Help**

📁 **Bookmarks Toolbar Folder**	▶
📁 **Condos**	▶
📁 **CPAP**	▶
📁 **Financial Links**	▶
📁 **Firefox and Mozilla Links**	▶
📁 **Illustrator book**	▶
📁 **Medical**	▶
📁 **Online Photo**	▶
📁 **PPINET sites**	▶
📁 **Quick Searches**	▶
📁 **Radio**	▶
📁 **Teaching**	▶
📁 **Writing Samples**	▶
📧 **ILLUSTRATOR GONE WILD!**	

CSS Layer Web Pages

Cascading style sheets (CSS) are the new wave in web page design because they offer more power and flexibility than HTML tables. CSS layers are stackable. They can be placed at absolute locations on a web page, and they are programmable with JavaScript.

The JavaScript element of working with CSS layers is way beyond the scope of this book. But here, however, I show you how to create the basic CSS layers for a portfolio web page with clickable thumbnails and a slideshow display of different images.

(1) Create a new file with RGB color, 800 pixels wide and 600 pixels high.

TIP

Debates over optimal web page width are endless, but for this project, you can assume visitors can handle an 800-pixel-wide site.

(2) In the Guides & Grid Preferences dialog box (choose Illustrator/Edit ➪ Preferences ➪ Guides & Grid), define gridlines every 60 pixels. Turn on View Grid and Snap to Grid from the View menu.

(3) One of your portfolio images on the page will be on the current layer. Name the current selected layer with a layer name that will help identify the image. This is for your reference (and to assist the JavaScript programmer who will be integrating your named layers into an interactive JavaScript application for a web site).

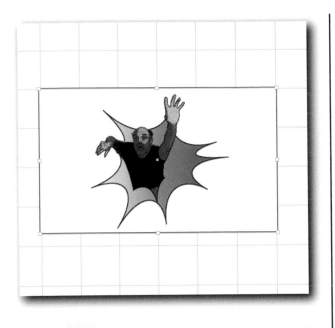

④ Place a second, third, and forth image on top of your original portfolio image. Make all four images about the same size. *Place each image in its own layer.*

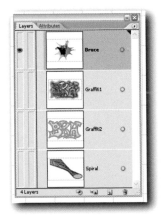

⑤ Before generating CSS, make all four layers visible. With your four layers visible, choose File ⇨ Save for Web. Choose JPEG from the Optimized File Format popup. Click the Layers tab in the Save for Web dialog box, and click the Export as CSS Layers checkbox. Select the first full layer you created in the Layer popup, and click the Preview Only Selected Layer checkbox. Define this layer as visible.

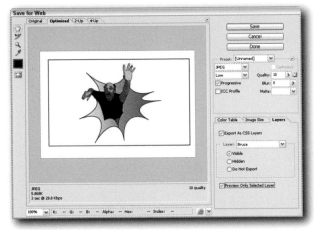

⑥ Select the second full layer you created in the Layer popup, and click the Preview Only Selected Layer checkbox. Define this layer as visible. Choose JPEG from the Optimized File Format popup.

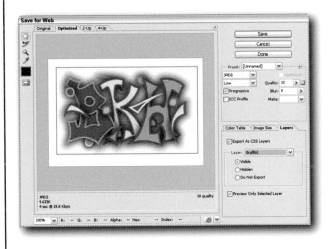

7 Make the two remaining full layers visible as well. Choose JPEG format for both of them.

8 Click Save in the Save for Web dialog box. The Save Optimized dialog box opens. Choose HTML and Images from the Save as Type popup, and enter an HTML filename in the File name box.

9 The web page is saved, with CSS layers and JPEG images in the layers. Programs such as Macromedia Dreamweaver or Adobe GoLive have tools that allow you to attach JavaScripts to the thumbnails to hide and display other full-sized images as visitors to your web site click on elements on the page that activate hide and display layer scripts.

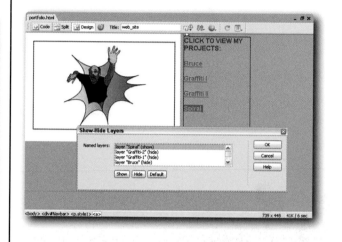

Glitches

I'm pushing the limits of Illustrator CS2's ability to generate CSS layers. The layers you create in Illustrator do not include CSS positioning attributes in a form that allows you to use them for page design. Absolute positioning on a page is a major element of how CSS layers are used for page design.

What you can do with Illustrator-generated CSS is create named layers, which can be hidden and displayed as a visitor interacts with a web page (for instance, by moving his or her mouse cursor over part of the page to change the display of another part of the page).

To see a large version of this graffiti type, turn the page.

10 When viewed in a browser, the JavaScript you generate in GoLive or Dreamweaver hides and reveals layers depending on how visitors interact with other elements on the page.

NOTE

You can see this page at www.illustratorgonewild.com/portfolio.html.

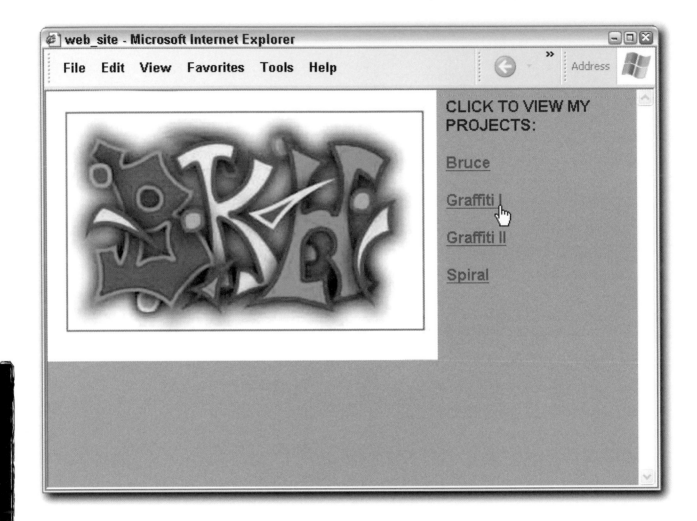

index

continued

index